Signature
of the Sun

SOUTHWEST VERSE, 1900 - 1950

Signature of the Sun

SOUTHWEST VERSE, 1900-1950

Selected and Edited by
MABEL MAJOR, *Texas Christian University*
T. M. PEARCE, *University of New Mexico*

THE UNIVERSITY OF NEW MEXICO PRESS
Albuquerque, New Mexico

Contents

Introduction

At a period in history when man has learned to peer into what was once considered the ultimate mystery of matter and to use this knowledge to change the very face of nature itself, one wonders whether society has greater or less need of poetry, once considered a primary source of mystery and a solution of fundamental problems in nature, such as bringing down rain, sending up crops, and curing men's illnesses. An answer can well be made from an area like the American Southwest where, within a distance of thirty miles, may be found today the world's greatest laboratory of atomic science and the world's oldest forms of poetic dance drama and word rituals.

Although this is a book of Southwest verse, the themes expressed and the forms employed are only to a limited degree regional. The poetry of Southwestern Indians, for instance, is representative of the poetry of Indians throughout the Americas. The Latin mood in folk poetry and in literary forms brings into American English the sentiment and imagery native to the Romance languages south of the Rio Grande. Anglo-American poetry in this region, though marked by nature and by human experience with distinctive regional accents, is still related to American folk traditions and to the literary stream of English and American poetry.

We hope to develop the individual character of Southwest verse in the various sections of the book. The arrangement has been determined partly by the way of life of peoples and partly by the geographical outlines of the region. The poets in the volume come from Arkansas, Texas, Oklahoma, New Mexico, and Arizona. Yet, in our organization of the materials, we proceed roughly in reverse of this east to west statement, beginning with the poetry of the oldest settlements, the Indian, in New Mexico and Arizona, and then proceeding by way of the verse about the Rio Grande country to the mirror which poetry holds up to nature on the plains and prairies, woodland and gulf. Nature conditioning man and man shaping nature are the basic statements of much of the poetry from this area of illimitable contrasts and extremes, unified by proximity and wind-crossed, earth-crossed trails. In the Southwest, oil booms from the earth by man's command, and then shapes a mold of machinery, rags to riches poverty-wealth, waste and abundance. The sky commands and is commanded. From the trackless sphere of air has come the inspiration for poems in one of our finest groups. And last, but with no intent of arrangement as climax, are poems of the personal way and the personal world of the individual poet.

The primitive and the modern Indian, the Spanish and the Anglo explorer, pioneer and settler, the rancher and the cowboy, the Negro worker and farmer, the wildcatter and the conservative oil man, all share the rhythm of daily life, the images in the eye, the labors of the hand, the vocabulary on the tongue. Their voices are heard in the poetry here. Voices too, have the housewife, the professional man, the aviator, the veterans of both world wars, the teacher, preacher, priest, men and women unclassified, singing of others or of themselves, alone with their thoughts in the universal spring or fall, heat or cold, pagan or religious mood, thinking of very personal things, home, neighborhood, loved ones. SIGNATURE OF THE SUN, we believe, bears a regional stamp, but we also believe that it bears the stamp of good poetry written in America.

MABEL MAJOR
T. M. PEARCE

2

PART I

Pueblo, Hogan and Tepee

Modern man cannot revert to primitive ways of life except in play or in brief, serious gesture, as Thoreau went to Walden wood. Yet the mind of a poet can be stimulated by the poetry of primitives and through the imagination comprehend something of simpler states of being and simpler art forms, for art has not always achieved its highest perfection in the most complex states of human society.

In the Southwest the oral tradition of poetry among such Indian groups as the sedentary Pueblos and the semi-nomadic Navajos and Apaches has been closely associated with pageantry and ceremonial. The oldest poetry of Indian groups has been a part of their effort by ceremonial art to reach a harmony with Nature and by this harmony to compel Nature to serve mankind. So the Indian imitates the fall of rain by his dance step; proclaims the call of thunder by his drum beat; reproduces images of growth by pine bough or gourd rattle. Choruses who accompany the corn dance with chanting send the word vibrating into the air, so that words become a compelling force potent with energy. Archibald MacLeish has said that "A poem should not mean but be." In the sense that a form of reality is incorporated in words, the Indian believes that poetry is an actual compelling thing, something more than words reflecting thoughts or symbols of meaning passing from mind to mind. In this section devoted to poetry by Indians or about Indians the reader will find material as ancient as the myth world and as modern as the world of the automobile.

One of the earliest Anglo-American interpreters of the Indian world in the Southwest was Albert Pike, a New Englander, who left the East when he was twenty-two years of age and came over the Santa Fe Trail to New Mexico. In *Prose Sketches and Poems* he leaves a number of impressions of Indians: "The Navajo Warrior" and "A Dirge" among them. Pike left Santa Fe in 1832 and no major treatment of the Indian theme occurred in the Southwest until Charles Poston of Arizona wrote *Apache Land* (1878), a long narrative poem which tells the story of a Spanish girl who was captured by Apaches and who became the wife of a chieftain. Later she went to Mexico and Europe in the company of the Empress Carlotta, and then returned as a Sister of the Sacred Heart to her people in Arizona. Although Poston was Superintendent of Indian Affairs in the territory, and knew the Apache country, his epic is more visionary than real and lacking in true feeling for the Indians as a people.

Contributors to "Pueblo, Hogan and Tepee" are, first, those who translate or re-express original Indian material and, second, those who interpret the Indian world in theme, imagery, and rhythms. The group dealing with original Indian poetry consists of such writers as Washington Matthews, Ruth Murray Underhill, Herbert Joseph Spinden, and Mary Austin. "A Prayer of the Night Chant" is a Navajo choral song expressing the earliest form of nature worship to heal and restore the sick soul and body. "Singing Up the Corn" shows how the Papago works with nature through sound, image, and gesture to promote growth. Both poems are translations, the first by Washington Matthews, authority on language, lore and ceremony, and the second by Ruth Murray Underhill, anthropologist with the U. S. Indian Service, who studied and lived in Southwest Indian communities, learning the tongues and folkways. The Tewa poem by Herbert Joseph Spinden is, also, an authentic transcription. Mary Austin called her Indian poems "re-expressions," because she worked with translators, using her gift of interpretation and drawing upon years of experience with Indian ways of life and thought. It is in this vein that Ina Sizer Cassidy transcribed her poem, "The Maid Who Became a Bear." After attending a Navajo "sing," she writes "I found an old Navajo medicine man who sang for me, and a young government employee who translated the words. After returning home I consulted Matthews, to check my material, which I found to be authentic."

The Indian, like every other race, has advanced through some individuals and in some places to contemporary civilization and the sophistication of learning. Too often in acquiring the civilization of the white man, he loses the genius native to him. John Rollins Ridge, a quarter-breed Cherokee, wrote poetry in the Southwest for a time. But it was in the Byronic vein. By contrast, the work of Alexander Posey, an educated Creek Indian of Oklahoma, is expressed in Indian imagery and reflects the Indian point of view. The style, however, is that of the white man's poetry. The Indian form, a kind of free verse disciplined by repetition of line and the pattern of phrasing, is faithfully shown in "Beauty," by Louise Abeita, a Pueblo Indian girl.

Anglo-Americans, writing as poets, and freed from the bond of translation or re-expression, have still tried to catch the thought, mood, and rhythm of the Indian poetic world. So, a primitive folk tradition has stimulated sophisticated art expression. "A Dance for Rain" by Witter Bynner, incorporates something of the Indian *beat, beat, beat* into its rhythm, shaping the primitive world into modern expression as poetry. Charles Beghtol and Haniel

Long approach the elemental forces directly with the simplicity of Indian address. Whitney Montgomery and Daisy Lemon Coldiron capture, imaginatively, the dilemma of Indians, from their first contacts with the white man's world: struggling with two cultures, one dying, the other not yet born for them. Paul Eldridge in "Gray Roadster" points a climax but no solution. Yet the problem is not entirely Indian. For, as Europeans have lived in America, an Indian land from frontier days to the present, they have acquired something of the Indian soul. What the Indians may have lost of beauty and serenity has been preserved in his poetry, and can be recaptured there. The reader will find proof of this from the poets who contribute to Section I of SIGNATURE OF THE SUN.

A PRAYER OF THE NIGHT CHANT

Navajo

Tsegihi.
House made of dawn.
House made of evening light.
House made of the dark cloud.
House made of male rain.
House made of dark mist.
House made of female rain.
House made of pollen.
House made of grasshoppers.
Dark cloud is at the door.
The trail out of it is dark cloud.
The zigzag lightning stands high upon it.
Male deity!
Your offering I make.
I have prepared a smoke for you.
Restore my feet for me.
Restore my legs for me.
Restore my body for me.
Restore my mind for me.
This very day take out your spell for me.
Your spell remove for me.
You have taken it away for me.
Far off it has gone.
Happily I recover.
Happily my interior becomes cool.
Happily I go forth.
My interior feeling cool, may I walk.
No longer sore, may I walk.
Impervious to pain, may I walk.
With lively feelings may I walk.
As it used to be long ago, may I walk.
Happily may I walk.
Happily, with abundant dark clouds, may I walk.

Happily, with abundant showers, may I walk.
Happily, with abundant plants, may I walk.
Happily, on a trail of pollen, may I walk.
Happily may I walk.
Being as it used to be long ago, may I walk.
May it be beautiful before me.
May it be beautiful behind me.
May it be beautiful below me.
May it be beautiful above me.
May it be beautiful all around me.
In beauty it is finished.

WASHINGTON MATTHEWS

SINGING UP THE CORN

Papago

Evening is falling.
Pleasantly sounding
Will reverberate
Our songs.

The corn comes up;
It comes up green;
Here upon our fields
White tassels unfold.

The corn comes up;
It comes up green;
Here upon our fields
Green leaves blow in the breeze.

Blue evening falls,
Blue evening falls;

Near by, in every direction,
It sets the corn tassels trembling.

The wind smooths well the ground.
Yonder the wind runs
Upon our fields.
The corn leaves tremble.

On Tecolote fields
The corn is growing green.
I came there, saw the tassels waving in the breeze,
And I whistled softly for joy.

Blowing in the wind,
Singing,
Am I crazy corn?

Blowing in the wind,
Singing,
Am I laughing corn?

The night moves, singing.
Not sleepy, I.
A stick I cut to represent the corn.
Where I find the yellow bees
There will be much corn.

A little yellow cricket
At the roots of the corn
Is hopping about and singing.

A little yellow cricket
At the roots of the squash
Is hopping about and singing.

[Corn speaks:]
The little striped woodpecker
Descends right down into my heart.

9

[Man speaks:]
This my bow
Twangs in the cornfield.

It moves in different directions,
It moves in different directions,
And then it alights
From the south,
On the blue water—
The dragonfly.

It moves in different directions,
It moves in different directions,
And then it stands still
From the south,
On the yellow water—
The dragonfly.

All together, all together they sing—
The red beans.
All together, all together they sing—
The white beans.

Am I not the magic tobacco?
Here I come forth and grow tall.
Am I not the magic tobacco?
The blue hummingbird finds my flowers.
Above them softly he is humming.

At last they sing the harvest song, as the corn of different
colors speaks from the harvester's arms.

Truly most comfortably you embrace me:
I am the blue corn.
Truly most comfortably you embrace me:
I am the red corn.

RUTH MURRAY UNDERHILL

BEAUTY

Beauty is seen
In the sunlight,
The trees, the birds,
Corn growing and people working
Or dancing for their harvest.

Beauty is heard
In the night,
Wind sighing, rain falling,
Or a singer chanting
Anything in earnest.

Beauty is in yourself.
Good deeds, happy thoughts
That repeat themselves
In your dreams,
In your work,
And even in your rest.

E-YEH-SHURE' (LOUISE ABEITA)

PAPAGO LOVE SONGS

I.

Early I rose
In the blue morning;
My love was up before me,
It came running to me from the doorways of the
        Dawn.

On Papago Mountain
The dying quarry
Looked at me with my love's eyes.

Do you long, my Maiden,
For bisnaga blossoms
To fasten in your hair?

I will pick them for you.
What are bisnaga spines to me
Whom love is forever pricking in the side?

MARY AUSTIN

LAMENT OF A MAN FOR HIS SON

Son, my son!

I will go up to the mountain
And there I will light a fire
To the feet of my son's spirit,
And there will I lament him;
Saying,
O my son,
What is my life to me, now you are departed!

Son, my son,
In the deep earth
We softly laid thee in a Chief's robe,
In a warrior's gear.
Surely there,
In the spirit land
Thy deeds attend thee!
Surely,
The corn comes to the ear again!

But I, here,
I am the stalk that the seed-gatherers

Descrying empty, afar, left standing.
Son, my son!
What is my life to me, now you are departed?

MARY AUSTIN

SONG FOR THE PASSING OF A BEAUTIFUL WOMAN

Strong sun across the sod can make
Such quickening as your countenance!

I am more worth for what your passing wakes,
Great races in my loins, to you that cry.
My blood is redder for your loveliness.

MARY AUSTIN

SONG OF THE SKY LOOM

Tewa

Oh our Mother the Earth, oh our Father the Sky,
Your children are we, and with tired backs
We bring you the gifts that you love.
Then weave for us a garment of brightness;
May the warp be the white light of morning,
May the weft be the red light of evening,
May the fringes be the falling rain,
May the border be the standing rainbow.
Thus weave for us a garment of brightness
That we may walk fittingly where birds sing,
That we may walk fittingly where grass is green
Oh our Mother the Earth, oh our Father the Sky!

HERBERT JOSEPH SPINDEN

THE MAID WHO BECAME A BEAR

The Maid who became a Bear walks far around.
On the Black Mountain she walks around,
In beauty she walks,
Far around in beauty she walks.

Far spreads the land,
It seems not far to her.
Dim shows the land,
It seems not dim to her.

On the Blue Mountain she walks around,
Far around she walks. Far spreads the land—
It seems not far to her, it seems not dim.
She walks around;
The fires blaze as she walks,
The mountains burn in her steps;
Smoke clouds rise high,
Smoke clouds curtain the sky;
As she walks the waters burn, the waters blaze.
Thus the Holy Maid seeks the gods and finds them:
On the mountain-peaks she seeks the gods
And finds them;
On the summits of the clouds, the floating clouds,
The red clouds,
She seeks the gods and finds them.
And so can we, so can we!
Let us go—it seems not far to us!
Let us go—it seems not dim to us!
Let us seek the gods and find them.

INA SIZER CASSIDY

ON A MARBLE MEDALLION OF DANTE

Close-hooded as a monk;
High-cheeked as a Red Man;
High-nosed as a Hebrew;
Full-lipped as a Greek God.

The character revealed
In this bit of white stone
Is such as is not stamped
Upon a human face
Once in a thousand years.

ALEXANDER L. POSEY

RED MAN'S PLEDGE OF PEACE

I pledge you by the moon and sun,
As long as stars their course shall run,
Long as day shall meet my view,
Peace shall reign between us two.

I pledge you by those peaks of snow
As long as streams to ocean flow,
Long as years their youth renew,
Peace shall reign between us two.

I came from mother soil and cave,*
You came from pathless sea and wave,
Strangers fought our battles through,—
Peace shall reign between us two.

ALEXANDER L. POSEY

*The Creeks have a legend about their having originated from the caves and earth.

TWO CLOUDS

Away out west, one day,
Two clouds were seen astray.
One came up from the sea,
    Afar unto the south,
And drifted wearily;
    One came out of the north.
Away out west that day,
A town was swept away.

ALEXANDER L. POSEY

ON THE CAPTURE AND IMPRISONMENT OF CRAZY SNAKE,* JANUARY, 1900

Down with him! chain him! bind him fast!
    Slam to the iron door and turn the key!
The one true Creek, perhaps the last
    To dare declare, "You have wronged me!"
Defiant, stoical, silent,
    Suffers imprisonment!

Such coarse black hair! such eagle eye!
    Such stately mien!—how arrow-straight!
Such will! such courage to defy
    The powerful makers of his fate!
A traitor, outlaw,—what you will,
    He is the noble red man still.

Condemn him and his kind to shame!
    I bow to him, exalt his name!

ALEXANDER L. POSEY

*Crazy Snake—Chitto Harjo. The leader of a band of Creeks who oppose the abolishment of their tribal rights. Several times Harjo has been imprisoned because of his defying the United States authorities.

BALLAD OF CYNTHIA ANN PARKER

You have brought me back to my people,
 Or so you would have me believe,
And you wonder why I am silent,
 And you wonder why I should grieve.

You say that I was a white child,
 A Paleface, born and bred;
If my blood is the blood of the White man,
 My heart is the heart of the Red.

You have spoken a name that strangely
 And vaguely comes back to me,
Like the faint perfume of a flower
 Or a long lost memory—

A name that haunts and mocks me
 Like the words of a half-heard song;
I wish that I might remember,
 But the years have been too long.

You tell me I should be happy
 Here with my people once more,
You would have me forget Nocona
 And the tall sons that I bore.

People? Who are my people?
 And what is this freedom to me?
Why should you prate of freedom
 Who have always slaughtered the free!

How can I ever forget
 The tepee fires at night,
The scent of the pines at evening,
 And dawn on the mountain height;

The endless leagues of flowers
   That the April winds unrolled,
And the countless buffalo herds
   That the white man slaughtered for gold;

And how can I ever forget
   The terror of that last ride,
When I clung to my flying pony
   And my baby clung to my side;

When they wounded my brave Nocona,
   And he leaned him against a tree,
Dying, but scorning the mercy
   That they proffered half-heartedly?

You have brought me back to my people,
   Or so you would have me believe,
And you wonder why I am silent,
   And you wonder why I should grieve.

You say that I was a white child,
   A Paleface, born and bred,—
If my blood is the blood of the White man,
   My heart is the heart of the Red!

                    WHITNEY MONTGOMERY

QUANAH HEARS TWO CALLS

The winds that blow in the Southland,
They talk and they talk to me;
Always I hear them calling,
Calling eternally:
Come to your Mother's people,
Come to your blood, your own!

I came . . .
And the winds that blow to the Southland
Are blowing new worlds to me.
They are blowing me words that are precious
And the God of the White-man Way;
But the wild, prairie winds are calling me,
And oh, I cannot stay!

> *(The wild, prairie winds are moaning,*
> *"Quanah, Quanah, why do you roam?"*
> *The winds of my fathers are calling me,*
>   *crying, calling me home.)*

The winds that blow in the Southland
Are blowing my Mother to me,
They are blowing me understanding
Of her that could never be free.
They are blowing me love for her people,
I could follow the White-man Way
But the wild, prairie winds are calling me,
And oh, I cannot stay!
The winds of my fathers are calling me,
They moan, they are never still,
And I must go back to the prairies,
And the last Sun-dance on the hill.

> *(For the wild, free winds are moaning:*
> *"Quanah, Quanah, why do you roam?"*
> *The winds of my fathers are calling,*
>   *ever they call me home.)*

The winds that blow in the Southland
Are blowing me Cynthia's love,
They blow me the White-man religion
And the great white spirit above.
But always above their murmur
I hear the wild winds moan—
Nacona, my Father, I hear you,

I am coming back to my own!
I hear you, my Father, calling:
"Come back to your own tepee!"
And I must go back to my people
Where they watch and wait for me.

(The long, strong winds are moaning:
"Quanah, Quanah, why do you roam?"
Oh the winds of my fathers are calling,
ever they call me home!)

DAISY LEMON COLDIRON

HANDS

Inside a cave in a narrow canyon near Tassajara
The vault of rock is painted with hands.
A multitude of hands in the twilight, a cloud of men's
        palms, no more,
No other picture. There's no one to say
Whether the brown shy quiet people who are dead
        intended
Religion or magic, or made their tracings
In the idleness of art; but over the division of years
        these careful
Signs-manual are now like a sealed message
Saying, "Look: we also were human; we had hands, not
        paws.
        All hail
You people with the cunning hands, our supplanters
In the beautiful country; enjoy her a season, her beauty,
        and come down
And be supplanted; for you also are human."

ROBINSON JEFFERS

20

HOPI PRAYER

Rain, lean down
And touch my lands,
For I have many mouths to feed.
Sunshine, give me both
Your hands
To lift the flowers I need.

Wind, blow gently
From the west,
My harvest time is near.
Spirit, Thou hast
Done thy best
To allay my fear.

CHARLES BEGHTOL

INDIANS

They wear squash-flowers cut in silver
And carve the sun on canyon walls;
Their words are born of storm and calyx,
Eagles, and waterfalls.

They weave the thunder in the basket,
And paint the lightning on the bowl:
Taking the village to the rainbow,
The rainbow to the soul.

HANIEL LONG

YO-TAN-E-KI

Study of a Cocapah Indian

Each day he sits and stares
Into the distance that is great,
And things are in his eyes
That words have puzzled to relate.

Coarse denim clothes him now,
A chambray shirt, and flop-eared hat
Which all but hides his eyes,
And wire-tied shoes worn thin and flat.

His knotted hands are still
Within his lap; resigned, it seems,
To idleness and age,
And to the vanishing of dreams.

His rounded shoulders droop
Like eagle's wings grown weak with flight
Far down an unknown sky
Where darkness is, and death, and night.

No sigh, no movement shows;
He might as well be sun-baked clay . . .
But in his staring eyes
Are things words were not meant to say.

D. MAITLAND BUSHBY

HOTEVILLA

The Indians dance for tourist trade
And speak an alien tongue
But dream of tattered years ago
When their tribe was young.

With stolid pride and bitter heart
They know the race is dying . . .
Religion, a commercial right
Gods are exercising.

NORMAN MACLEOD

SANTO DOMINGO

I. The Girls Are Dancing

"Let me wear your beads, Mother. I want to dance," the
    girl said.
"All right," the Indian mother answered,
And she took the turquoise from around her head.

Underneath the cottonwoods to the beat of a drum—
Underneath the umbrella of the clouds—
The girl moved softly with tablita bowed
Now to the east and now to the west,
Now to the south and now to the north—
Commanding the raindrops to come forth.

And the clouds were not angry, nor was the wind,
For her dance was subtle and her song was sweet
As raindrops splashing upon her feet.

But if it had not been for her mother
And the turquoise beads so perfectly strung,
And all her sisters dancing in unison
And the men who were beating upon the drum,
The rain would never have come so soon!

For this we thank you. And thanks again!

II. *From Cutting the Wheat*

"We thank you and thanks again," the Santo Domingoes
    say
In their song when returning from cutting the wheat—
And every object of the turquoise world is peaceful, it
    seems—
Even the tassels of wheat are colored with dreams.
And after the slender copper threads of the wheat are cut,
They are soft and flaxen as the hair on a girl's head.
Even the wheatfields seem happy with their new haircut—
But most of all the Indians are at peace, it seems!
(For grain stacked in the pueblo makes good dreams)—

But before the cutting the people of the field were gay:
"The wheat was getting excited!" the Santo Domingoes
    say.

III. *Working in the Corn*

We are working in the fields where crops are growing—
For we are helping the Corn People,
Whose ears turn yellow in the sun—

An Indian makes his fire at noon and says,
"Come over and have lunch with me!"
And the others say, "Let's go over there
And have lunch with him!"

But first the spirit must be fed—
Or else the Corn People might feel bad!
"I wish it would rain!" they say.

We hope the clouds in the west will come our way,
For we are working for the whole people
And not for ourselves alone, we say.

While into the turquoise sky
The yellow cornstalks climb—

We thank the clouds. We thank them all the time!

NORMAN MACLEOD

A DANCE FOR RAIN

Cochiti

You may never see rain, unless you see
A dance for rain at Cochiti,
Never hear thunder in the air
Unless you hear the thunder there,
Nor know the lightning in the sky
If there's no pole to know it by.
They dipped the pole just as I came,
And I can never be the same
Since those feathers gave my brow
The touch of wind that's on it now,
Bringing over the arid lands
Butterfly gestures from Hopi hands
And holding me, till earth shall fail,
As close to earth as a fox's tail.

I saw them, naked, dance in line
Before the candles of a leafy shrine:
Before a saint in a Christian dress
I saw them dance their holiness,
I saw them reminding him all day long
That death is weak and life is strong
And urging the fertile earth to yield
Seed from the loin and seed from the field.
A feather in the hair and a shell at the throat
Were lifting and falling with every note
Of the chorus-voices and the drum,
Calling for the rain to come.
A fox on the back, and shaken on the thigh
Rain-cloth woven from the sky,
And under the knee a turtle-rattle
Clacking with the toes of sheep and cattle—
These were the men, their bodies painted
Earthen, with a white rain slanted;

These were the men, a windy line,
Their elbows green with a growth of pine.
And in among them, close and slow,
Women moved, the way things grow,
With a mesa-tablet on the head
And a little grassy creeping tread
And with sprays of pine moved back and forth,
While the dance of the men blew from the north,
Blew from the south and east and west
Over the field and over the breast.
And the heart was beating in the drum,
Beating for the rain to come.

Dead men out of earlier lives,
Leaving their graves, leaving their wives,
Were partly flesh and partly clay,
And their heads were corn that was dry and gray.
They were ghosts of men and once again
They were dancing like a ghost of rain;
For the spirits of men, the more they eat,
Have happier hands and lighter feet,
And the better they dance the better they know
How to make corn and children grow.

And so in Cochiti that day,
They slowly put the sun away
And they made a cloud and they made it break
And they made it rain for the children's sake.
And they never stopped the song or the drum
Pounding for the rain to come.

The rain made many suns to shine,
Golden bodies in a line
With leaping feather and swaying pine.
And the brighter the bodies, the brighter the rain
Where thunder heaped it on the plain.
Arroyos had been empty, dry,
But now were running with the sky;

And the dancers' feet were in a lake,
Dancing for the people's sake.
And the hands of a ghost had made a cup
For scooping handfuls of water up;
And he poured it into a ghostly throat,
And he leaped and waved with every note
Of the dancers' feet and the songs of the drum
That had called the rain and made it come.

For this was not a god of wood,
This was a god whose touch was good,
You could lie down in him and roll
And wet your body and wet your soul;
For this was not a god in a book,
This was a god that you tasted and took
Into a cup that you made with your hands,
Into your children and into your lands,
This was a god that you could see,
Rain, rain, in Cochiti!

WITTER BYNNER

MISSISSIPPI INDIANS

The children used to tell me tales of how
    The Indians once came marching single-file
    Past the Big House. They stopped a little while
To drink the cold spring-water, running now
As then, from underneath the low-hung bough
    Of an old sycamore that stood a mile
    From the main traveled road, but near the pile
Of the plantation houses crowning the brow

Of a small hill that overlooked the place.
    Imagination pictured painted braves
    On the warpath! The eagle plume that waves
In fierce defiance over each savage face!
    But now I know those Indians walked with fears
    A pilgrimage they named The Trail of Tears.

ANNE McCLURE

IN PETERBOROUGH WOODS

    Chief of the Mohawks
    Going Snake
    On the warpath
    Wearing his war paint
    And eagle-feather bonnet
    Received a poisoned arrow in his breast.

    Unfaltering he turned
    And sped into the forest;
    There, in solitude,
    In decent privacy,
    Laid aside his hurt body
    As his brother snake his skin,
    And went forth to another hunting ground.

    Having come from far
    Here I might cast this body
    Like Going Snake;
    And without ritual,
    With no funeral drums
    Or tardy-falling tears
    Or lying eulogy
    Begin again!

ANNE McCLURE

BLANKET FLOWERS

It was on a June morning, on a Sunday morning early
    That, as I went walking, I walked in Brattle Street.
Birds in the Cambridge elms were singing very clearly
    And from the Charles River the wind was soft and
        sweet.

Old fashioned flowers in the gardens nodded gravely,
    Larkspur and roses and red hollyhocks,
And one lone gaillardia was smiling very bravely
    Among the day lilies and the purple standing phlox.

Gaillardias are blanket flowers on the Caddo Reservation,
    And I know a valley that the blanket flowers fill,
As big as all of Cambridge, by Old Caddo Station
    Between a little river and a long sand hill.

The wild wind of the prairie shakes the sage brush above it,
    And spotted Indian ponies go straggling one by one
To drink at the river, and the meadow larks love it,
    And the blanket flowers are blazing in the Oklahoma
      sun.

                       KENNETH C. KAUFMAN

ALIBI

Six foot two in his moccasins,
    Stately, unbowed with age,
Eagle Bull came down the sun-parched street,
    And I questioned the old Osage.

29

For the drouth was sore in the country.
"When will it rain? Can you say?"
He nodded. "Rain pretty soon," he said,
"Hoot owl holler in day."

But the days went on and it still was dry,
And I said to the chief, "Oho!
What about rain?" "I mistake," he said.
"That was young owl. He don't know!"

ZOE A. TILGHMAN

NE-SHA-BE*

Dark Water

Winds on Ne-sha-be calling, softly calling,
Crying their endless quest;
Nor shall the Night, on the dark water falling,
Bring answer from the west.

Ever the winds upon Ne-sha-be blowing,
And the white wave's crest,
When you and I are passed beyond its knowing—
Lie in the dark Earth's breast.

Winds on Ne-sha-be, ever the long tryst keeping
Stay not the stern behest;
But thou and I and our love forever sleeping,
Shall by the Dark Water, rest!

ZOE A. TILGHMAN

*Ne, "water," in Osage and other Indian languages of the Siouan stock. Always placed first, as Nebraska, *Neosho. Sha-be,* "dark."

IN THE OSAGE COUNTRY

The gray humps of hills walk into the morning.
Wrapped in gray blankets they move
Heavily to the sky;
To the sky where the dawn is
Orange lilies and roses
Like a print from old Japan.
But this is Osage, not yellow China.
On the streets of Pawhuska
Copper colored Indians in rainbow blankets
Are standing like jack-oaks in a sunset.
From the old rock council house
A wisp of smoke floats
To the hill where Texas Silk Johnny
Was hanged for a cattle rustler;
Hanged, while Indians in rainbow blankets
Watched solemnly, like jack-oaks in autumn.

HENRY T. CHAMBERS

CREEKS

These men forsook one culture for another.
Their fathers' fathers
Fought for the white man's civilization.
They have been
Baptized in blood at the battle of Bird Creek.
But that was long ago and now
It is Saturday night in Bristow, in the Creek Nation.
Hovering in store doorways,
Shoved carelessly by white men and Negroes,
Elbowed by Freedmen,

The Creeks, ragged and bewildered,
Count their pennies, buy calico and potatoes,
And prod a team of mules from a rickety wagon
To take them back to God-knows-where.

HENRY T. CHAMBERS

GRAY ROADSTER

On seeing a gray sport roadster at the Oklahoma Automobile Show bearing on the windshield the inscription: "Bought by — (a well-known young Osage Indian)."

I wonder what ditch in northeastern Oklahoma
You will presently adorn, slim gray roadster . . .
Will the slim young Osage who steers you
Snuff you out some flaring night
When the cars roar deep-throated
Down the Bartlesville road?
Or will he destroy you by day
In a flowering plum thicket,
Intoxicating in its perfume?
(There are plum trees at every curve of the road
In his country.)

Is your steel more sturdy,
Are your fibers more felted
Than those of the eight Nashes and the Paige
Who preceded you in the hands of the indefatigable
      destroyer—

The slim young Osage?
Will he release you, too—
Leap lightly as a cat from your body
In the ever-present crisis?
Or will you kill him?

Perish together to the pulsations of a power-house,
The mutter of a gas-torch,
The soft blows of a night-wind,
You, wrenched and stoical,
He, twisted and cursing,
With the fumes of gasoline and whisky in the soft
    night air?

For I see menace in the lines of you;
There is a smooth insolence about your beauty
Equal to his.
There should be written on your hood the name
    Nemesis—
Not *Lincoln*.

I wonder what ditch in northeastern Oklahoma
You will presently adorn, slim gray roadster!

PAUL ELDRIDGE

PART II

Along the Rio Grande

Age is the impression the Rio Grande country makes upon the visitor, age expressed in both nature's work and man's. In *Midnight on the Desert,* J. B. Priestly wrote, "The Southwest cannot be described in terms of history. By day it is geologic, and by night it is astronomic." All that is visible in nature spells out illimitable age, the earth and the enveloping bowl of the sky. It is not surprising that poets strive to put into words such timeless wonders as the Carlsbad Caverns, Monument Valley, and the Petrified Forest; or that thoughts should be provoked by the apparent history in ancient paths which men have walked and in the walls where they have long dwelt.

Time has moved beside a river in this region, the Rio Grande. Indian pueblo, Spanish town, American city mark its banks and draw sustenance from it. The Rio Grande is a great fountain in the heart of the sun-flooded land, and the trails of men lead to it, from it, and across it, when they do not follow the course from feeder streams in southern Colorado to Gulf far to the south. The greatest of these routes was, and is, the Santa Fe Trail, a land link between the Rio Grande and the Missouri. Poets were born on the Trail, spiritually born, that is. And in the desert stretches between the river basins men made their homes and learned to feel as deeply for these arid places as they had felt for wooded hills or meadowlands. Poetry grows wherever man's spirit is fed.

The New Mexico-Arizona group of poets in this section of SIGNATURE OF THE SUN consists of native-born or bred poets like Sharlot Hall, S. Omar Barker, and Fray Angelico Chavez; of indwellers like Alice Corbin Henderson, who pioneered the new poetry in Santa Fe three years after she and Harriet Monroe had founded *Poetry, a Magazine of Verse,* in Chicago, in 1918; of visitors who stayed long enough to become a part of the life although they did not always remain, like John Gould Fletcher, D. H. Lawrence, Charles Beghtol, and Lynn Riggs.

Santa Fe in the 1920's was a veritable mecca for poets, perhaps because Alice Corbin Henderson lent encouragement to youthful aspirants to the laurel and shared the fellowship of established writers, like Witter Bynner, Haniel Long, Mary Austin, and John Gould Fletcher, the latter an almost continuous summer resident in this period. Carl Sandburg, Vachel Lindsay, Robert Frost, Alfred Kreymborg and Maurice Leseman were among the poet-visitors to Santa Fe, participating, if they happened to be there, in The Poets' Roundup, the annual get-together started by Mrs. Henderson in 1929. This was a summer assembly, at which poets read their verses to an audience, and it was handled like a rodeo, with the poets the entertainers, instead of show horses, and a corral master to call the turns of each in the ring. The whole affair was both serious and semi-humorous, but the casual Western dress guaranteed an informal platform manner, and though the setting was usually someone's beautiful patio garden, the occasion never became a social rather than a truly creative activity. Langdon Mitchell, Thomas Wood Stevens, Ernest Thompson Seton, Lynn Riggs, Peggy Pond Church, Spud Johnson, John Curtis Underwood, S. Omar Barker, Fray Angelico Chavez, and visiting poets joined Austin, Bynner, Long and Henderson on these varied occasions between 1929 and 1939. The beginning of World War II ended The Poets' Roundup and ended, also, another unique project in Santa Fe. This was the co-operative publishing enterprise called Writers' Editions, which was organized by writers themselves to support limited editions of books. Between 1932 and 1939 Writers' Editions guided through the press nine titles of which eight were poetry. Suggested by the Poets' Roundup, a Poets' Conference was held in Albuquerque on August 13, 1940, as part of the Coronado Cuarto Centennial. Participating were Dorothy B. Hughes, Fray Angelico Chavez, Farona Konopak, Margaret Lohlker, Allison Ross, Alice Gill Benton, Ina Sizer Cassidy, Irene Fisher, Elizabeth Willis DeHuff, Ruth Cunningham, Dorothy Linney, Ethel M. Cheney, and Tom Boggs.

Local publishing during this period was active, too, in Texas, where Kaleidograph press and *Kaleidograph* poetry magazine were started by Whitney and Vaida Montgomery. More of the Texas poets who write of scenes along the Rio Grande are native to that state. John Houghton Allen, the Montgomerys, Arthur M. Sampley, Berta Hart Nance possess the land as a birthright. But more than birth is required to own a place in imagination and understanding. Sometimes the stranger, perceiving contrasts in a region rather than what is familiar, portrays it in a light the native would never see. But all poets are born of the spirit, and their growth is measured by the fruit they bear. Goldie Capers Smith, Fay M. Yauger, Patrick Dacus Moreland and others who were transplanted to the land of cactus, yucca blades, and Spanish names became identified with adopted soil through their poetry.

To some the strangeness still remained the stamp of poetry, the exotic quality in lands and progress, south and west. Strangeness and identification, then, are two dominant moods for poets along the Rio Grande. To the writer not born in the region, the contrasts make the strongest sensory appeal. To the native born or naturalized, the strange has become familiar, and the imagination kindles from insights of a deeper sort. Themes tied to place, to local custom, to historic deed and character stand out in this grouping of poems drawn from the five state area. Occasionally, a poet asks, "What significance for America has life along the Rio Grande? 'Eagle of the Rockies . . . What bird are you, in the end?'" Can anyone give a better answer than the poets?

To the Memory of Gerald Cassidy, Artist

I.

PUEBLO SONG

Wind-chased,
Wind-harried,
With the wind the world begins—
Wind whirling the white dust
Over the desert sands:
Wind-consumed,
Wind-eaten,
Wind has brought us foolish talk;
Wind has taken away the title of our lands.

Out of the south
Came buffalo going;
Winter has lost,
The snowdrift quits the plain;
Beast breath heats up
The slopes, long frozen;
Thunder is pushing against the wall of mountain,
Spring has come again.

Wind whirling
Wind whining,
Wind spinning up a cone of yellow dust
Beside the road.
Wind moving eastward;
The wild plum in blossom,
And the backs now more ready
To shoulder their load.

Out of the east
Rode the hard-bitten horsemen;

Rifles held ready,
Wagons creaking by.
The sage brush is trampled,
The antelope startled,
And the war-eagle
Forgets to watch his sky.

Wind quiet,
Wind lapsing,
Wind lifting no more the flap in the doorway,
Wind speaking to man no more.
Heat broods above the rooftops;
The blue-brown desert smoulders,
And the child that laughed here
Stands no longer at our door.

Out of the North
Ran howling the blizzard,
And over its fury
Came the roar of iron wheels;
And the hoot of long whistles
Through the barren hill-country:
Man's heart must be broken—
Yet the broken heart yields.

Wind howling,
Wind whooping,
Wind roaring,
Laughter without an end;
Down, down into darkness—
Like the pine cut and staggering,
Death, the sole answer,
Death, man's only friend.

Out of the west, now
Night on night the sunset;
Fingers of God moving
Up through the peaks afar.

Past without future,
Word without an answer,
Wind without meaning,
Man without a star:

Wind working,
Wind creeping,
Wind changing,
Wind cutting the flesh to bone.
God's breath against man's breath:
Souls adrift on the whirlwind,
Earth turned to desert—
Dust and the stars, alone.

II.

RIO GRANDE

Where the hummingbird hangs in the heat,
Where the blue thundercloud settles,
From the lips of the mountains blown forward,
Dark fringes of rain;
Where the dry canyon bed opens wide,
With its dark-green stunted cedars,
Shallow and turbid, seething and swift,
After the rapid rains;—
There will we wander,
Watching the shadows drift across the peaks,
By the Rio Grande,
That wild west river.

Where the pale brown adobe walls
Ranked into terraces, keep still their secret dreams;
Where the dark people peer shyly
Under their glossy black hair;
Where beneath from the depths of the kiva,
Comes the low chant and the loud drone of the
    drums,
Where through the sleepy plaza

Spin dust-whirls summoning the distant rains,
There will we dance,
As Gods holding high the world in our hearts,
By the Rio Grande,
That mad, swift river.

Where the *acequia* goes bank-full,
By the slopes of the burning grey desert,
Bearing to fields of green corn,
Tasseled and waving,
Its precious freight;
Where hollyhocks stand ranked high
Amid golden mullen, blue larkspur,
Where blue alfalfa burns deep,
Tempting bees to their honeyed fate,
There we will dream
Of a laugh, of a kiss, of a silence,
By the Rio Grande,
That dark and turbulent river.

Where the night with its wild blaze of stars
Stands still over lonely *mesas*,
And the earth is pressed close to the breast
Of the dark that abides beyond years;
Where all things are crumbling slowly,
The stone, the dream and the effort;
Where dogs from some unseen village
Bay loudly to the white moon;
There will we die,
Ebbing like flame from the Milky Way,
Blown smoke of the stars
From the breast wracked with pain,
By the Rio Grande,
The vast immutable River.

JOHN GOULD FLETCHER

CARLSBAD CAVE

As children, fearfully, we enter here,
To find a world incredible, unknown,
Where frozen fancies of the gnomes uprear
Their freakish forms, and beauty dreams in stone;
Where there are pale frost-gardens of delight,
And pools on which the sun has never gleamed,
With cells and chambers of primeval night,
Heights and abysms such as Dante dreamed;
And man has fenced a little space with flame,
Which his frail kind may safely wander through,
Old man and girl, small boy and portly dame,
And shrink from falling drops of earthy dew.

Step gently, folk, nor raise your voices here,
The living centuries are standing near.

BERTA HART NANCE

PETRIFIED FOREST

Arizona

If the dead should walk some desert night,
Strange men of shaggy limb
Would prowl here in a phantom light,
Misty and damp and dim;

Crouch and creep through the jungled wood
Of an ancient, vanished day,
In a shadowed marsh where tall trees stood
That never should know decay.

Not by fire nor ax nor saw
    Were these tall forests smitten.
No beavers' teeth were there to gnaw
    Them down. Their tale is written

Only in Time's unlettered scroll,
    By the lap of a turgid wave
That sealed hard beauty in each hole,
    And left them to their grave.

Broken wood on a desert plain,
    That grew in a primal mist:
Onyx and hyacinth in its grain,
    Agate and amethyst!

Listen! Tonight the desert wind,
    Dusting a moonlit sky,
Whispers of tourists, shaggy skinned,
    Out where the stone trees lie!

               S. OMAR BARKER

MONUMENT VALLEY

These are the mighty monuments that rise
To show the Gods' eternal resting place;
They weathered not the test of time or space,
That test which kills or does immortalize;
Perhaps the deity of angry skies
Sleeps, all forgotten, here; no legends trace
His stormy path to peace, for years erase
With gentle hand and pity in their eyes.

Gone myth and legend, all that fear controls;
We see with careless eyes where spirit dwelt—
And yet a holiness profound is there,
The sense of something sacred fills our souls,
The presence of the one great God is felt
Upon the stillness of the desert air.

LOU ELLA ARCHER

CORONADO CAME ON HORSEBACK

from Westward Under Vega

Coronado came on horseback,
Long and loud his trumpets blew
(But he couldn't hear the flute notes),
And his iron armor clattered
And the wary red folk scattered
Where his haughty banners flew.
(But he couldn't hear the mute notes
That had died before the flute notes—
Couldn't hear and never knew.)

General Kearney came with snare drums
And with bugles blowing strong
(But he couldn't hear the vespers),
And he made prophetic speeches
All of peace, as history teaches,
For his flag could do no wrong;
(But he couldn't hear the vespers,
Couldn't hear the quiet vespers'
Never ending evensong.)

Now you come with eights and sixes,
Brakes that squeal and horns that blow
(But you'll never hear the silence),
And the lizards know you're coming
When they hear your motors humming
And your gears go into low.
(But you'll never hear the silence—
Far too wide the desert silence,
Far too still the mountain silence
Ever such as you to know.)

Better sound your horn and go.

THOMAS WOOD STEVENS

PASÓ POR AQUÍ

Inscription Rock

I.

"Passed by here"—names on a rock
Oñate and de Vargas, Arrasain.

Names on a rock—
Luján and Nieto, Martínez.

II.

The winds carve a rock sign
And ride on, shouting.

The rains leave a sound of grass growing,
And fade into mist wisps.

Sunlight, moonlight, shine of stars,
Leave a remembrance with climbing cliffs.

III.

But your memorials, O my soul,
What are they?

They are as windblown dreams
That fade into mist wisps.

They are as the years that Time pours
From a cup brim full.

"Passed by this way"—
Only that is remembered.

WILLIAM HASKELL SIMPSON

SEVEN SONG

The Seven Towns of Cibola
Live only in a poet's rhyme;
A song has kept the walls of Troy
Against the somber siege of time.

A song can raise a mummied king
Of Egypt's dim and ancient land,
Launch purple sails upon the Nile,
Or ring the bells of Samarkand.

A poet's brief and golden lay
Within the tavern of a town,
At dawn can raise a Babylon—
At midnight hurl it down.

PATRICK DACUS MORELAND

LOS PENITENTES

I heard twelve *Penitentes* sing
A day that should have welcomed spring,
But all their path of pain was iced,
And every tree a white robed Christ;
And from the hilltop where I stood
I saw the snow a-spot with blood
That dripped from backs devout and bare,
And whipped, lest Hell their souls ensnare.

The time was when spring should have been
That twelve dark faced, barefooted men
Trudged chanting up their Holy Hill . . . .
The earth was white, the air was chill. . . .

Beneath some load I saw them stoop,
And every Christ-tree seemed to droop.
A cross rose up against the sky. . . .
I heard them chanting, wild and high. . . .

Then through the snow I hurried down
To my own fireside in the town.
'Tis such a somber, heart-break thing
When winter stays to haunt the spring.

                                    S. OMAR BARKER

JIM BRIDGER

All carelessly we travel o'er
        The ways he trod alone;
The noisy wheels send forth their roar
Where he stood on that gleaming shore
        And watched the salt waves thrown.

He saw the geysers gush on high,
    Where gleam red canyon walls;
He saw the circling seagulls fly
Where all in vain the salmon try
    To breast the thund'rous falls.

He scaled yon pass long ere the rails
    Lay glistening on the heights;
Perhaps his wraith takes up those trails
And roams, until the starlight fails,
    Through long and silent nights.

ARTHUR CHAPMAN

BEN MILAM

"Who will follow old Ben Milam
To San Antonio?
The Mexicans have taken the town
And hold the Alamo."

"But we have orders to retreat—"
"Retreat and be damned," he said.
"Who will follow old Ben Milam
And give them a fight instead?"

Three hundred men have volunteered
To go where Milam leads;
Three hundred men have armed themselves
For their heroic deeds.

Three hundred men have stormed the town
(Ben Milam leads the way);
And rifles sing their song of death
Upon this battle day.

"Lead on, Ben Milam, we follow you!"
But bloody and cold he lies,
Fallen there in the plaza dust
With a bullet between his eyes.

"Who will follow old Ben Milam,"
Were the words of his failing breath;
And there were heroes to follow him
Even unto death.

A. L. CROUCH

ALAMO

The city ebbs around her walls of stone;
Haggard and old, she muses, as the stream
Flows by, oblivious, "Why stand alone
To guard the phantom of a perished dream?"
From out the pulsing throng that knows no curb
There comes a little lad with careful tread,
His footfall gentle lest he might disturb
The peace of fallen heroes, long since dead.

Small hands caress the gray historic wall,
He turns to whisper, "Father, it was here
That Travis stood," the muted accents fall
To stir the waiting shadows far and near;
The hoary mission flings her challenge high:
"For such as he, my dreams shall never die!"

GOLDIE CAPERS SMITH

SAN JACINTO BATTLEFIELD

There is too much repose in this bright place
For bloodshed to have been . . . Today, serene
Soft shadows drift, and there is too much grace
In waving Spanish moss, in shining green
Upgrowth, in blue bayou, to reconcile
This peace with war. Yet, on this field the foe
Was overcome by Texas' rank and file
Of heroes but a century ago.

They fought on such a day as this, when fields
Held out on every side their wealth of bloom;
When earth gave promise of abundant yields
Of beauty indescribable,—a loom
On which the weaver's fingers could but play.
It was no easy thing to die that day.

NANCY RICHEY RANSON

SOUTHWEST

I could sing the lay of the broad paved way,
For I've travelled fast and far;
I have known the feel of the throbbing wheel
And the thrill of a racing car.

I could chant with glee of the wintry sea,
Where the great ships toss and roll;
Of the white-winged planes on the airy mains
Where the storm-gods take their toll.

But I've caught the zest of the Great Southwest,
In the realm of the rolling sand,
Where the lonesome note of the wild coyote
Floats over the Rio Grande.

So I'll tell the tale of the new-blazed trail,
Where the last frontier is won,
Where a man may ride at his partner's side
Right into the setting sun.

And I'll catch the tune of the desert's croon
As she hums in the blazing glow,
Hear the cowboy's song as he rides along
On the road to Mexico.

You may write the rimes of your gilded times,
And may take the fame it brings,
But I'll do my best by the Great Southwest
In the land of the Cattle Kings.

So I'm going home where the horned-toads roam,
And the glistening rattlers glide;
And I'll build me a shack in the blizzard's track
And buy me a horse to ride.

                                        LILITH LORRAINE

THE SANTA FE TRAIL

It winds o'er prairie and o'er crest,
      And tracks of steel now glance
Where once it lured men to the West,
      The highway of Romance.

Its furrows now are overgrown
      With snowdrift or with flower;
Lost are the graves so thickly sown
      By Death in that dim hour.

But when the night has drawn its veil
      The teams plod, span on span,
And one sees o'er the long dead trail
      A ghostly caravan.

                                        ARTHUR CHAPMAN

LINES FROM ARIZONA

I. Give Me New Words

Give me new words to tell of this land!
Do not let them sing, for it is a land too harsh for song;
Let them be hard as the black volcanic peaks,
Give me words as clear as the strange blue desert sky,
Let them shine as the fierce desert sun!

II. Arizona Mocking-Bird

Bird of the Louisiana magnolias,
How can you live—here?

Bird of the Texas prairies,
How can you sing—here?

III. Do Not Call Me

Do not call me to look at the mountains,
Eternal, indifferent,
Wrapping their veils of amethyst or violet about them,
Walking in cruel splendor across a land that is wracked
    and bare,—

Do not call me when the sun rises upon them,—
When the sun sets,—
Call me when the fog rises,
Letting me stand once more on my native prairie!

IV. Yaqui Dancers

Yaqui dancers,
Brown as pecan nuts, straight of limb,
Bare to the hips,
Take small steps with bent knees,
Flourish bronzed gourds in their slim hands,
Jingle the line of snake-rattles around their ankles,
Pace to the faint music of the Indian flute, the sticks
    rubbed together, the water-drums.
Above them shines the naked desert sky, saturated with
    sunlight,

Before them stretch the knobby foothills, spiked with
     giant cactus,
Farther away lies the long mottled bar of lilac mountain.
The dancers move in a checkered oval of tourists,
     university students, townsmen,
A girl over there watches with her lipstick raised and her
     mouth open,
The camera men are grinding hurriedly.
And I look—I look through the dancers to centuries that
     are dust.
Behind them the door of the past is ajar,
The cold breath that seeps from it brings a whisper of
     unutterable things,—
And my heart pounds and my nerves tremble!

V. San Xavier

I walked through the church of San Xavier,
With its baptismal font made of one piece of hammered
     copper,
The cord of Saint Francis encircling its walls,
Its high altar covered with gold leaf to the ceiling.

I saw the dome made by a famous Spanish architect,
And its border, designed and painted by the Papago
     Indians,
I saw the figures of the eleven apostles—the heart-breaking
     niche made for Judas and left vacant,
And the couchant wooden lions—in honor of the King
     of Spain—guarding the altar,
I saw the figures of small angels, among them an
     Indian angel, a Mexican angel,
And I saw—high up—on either side of the altar
The two great angels in silken robes that swing there,
And I was told that they were made as likenesses of the
     architect's two lovely daughters.
Forever young, forever beautiful, they smile down upon
     the visitor.

Then I thought of the flesh-and-blood women who lived
    long ago in Spain,
Laughing girls, given in marriage, bearing children,
    meeting the travail of life,
Growing old, dying, turning to dust—.
Yes, they have been dust now for over a century.
And I looked again at the angels, forever smiling, forever
    fair.

VI. Rodeo Parade

I stood on the sidewalk in Tucson,
Between a Papago Indian and a Mexican gentleman from
    the state of Sonora,
On the red-letter day of Arizona's year.
I saw the governor pass,
Riding in a state carriage built in Paris for Porfirio Diaz;
I saw Indians with long hair, dressed in native costume,
    playing white man's music on white man's instru-
    ments,
I saw an Indian chief in buckskin and feathers, riding a
    beautiful white horse,
I saw university girls in riding breeches, mounted on sleek
    horses with their manes cropped,
Scout bands, high school bands, the university band, two
    army bands,
I saw miners, cotton growers, cowboys, cowgirls, business
    men—.
They went by to the tramp of horses and the blare of
    music.
I saw Arizona: her eyes are as blue as the desert sky,
And her hair is the color of her copper sunsets,
Her garments are woven of the feathers of the palo verde,
On her head is a crown of stars,
And in her hands are healing and happiness.

BERTA HART NANCE

IN OLD TUCSON

Within a 'dobe wall,
In yonder desert, sere and bare,
While purple shadows of the night
Were falling everywhere,
And on the air, so soft and warm,
Faintly came the night-bird's call,
I left her standing there,
Amid the flowers, within a 'dobe wall
In Old Tucson.

Her eyes were dark as pools
In shaded desert wells;
Her words were like the tones
Of far-off mission bells;
The jet-black hue of night
Was on her glorious hair,
And still within that garden
I seem to see her—there
In Old Tucson.

And often in my dreams
She stands within a patio
In Old Tucson, where 'dobe walls
Were builded low;
And in a garden rare the hollyhocks
Grow straight and tall,
Within a 'dobe wall,
Where purple shadows slanting fall—
In Old Tucson.

CHARLES BEGHTOL

MEXICAN QUARTER *from* Arizona Poems

By an alley lined with tumble-down shacks,
And street-lamps askew, half-sputtering,
Feebly glimmering on gutters choked with filth and
    dogs
Scratching their mangy backs:
Half-naked children are running about,
Women puff cigarettes in black doorways,
Crickets are crying.
Men slouch sullenly
Into the shadows:
Behind a hedge of cactus,
The smell of a dead horse
Mingles with the smell of bacon-fat frying.

And a girl in a black lace shawl
Sits in a rickety chair by the square of an unglazed
    window,
And sees the explosion of the stars
Softly poised on the velvet sky.
And she is humming to herself:—
"Stars, if I could reach you
(You are so very clear that it seems as if I could
    reach you),
I would give you all to the Madonna's image,
On the grey-plastered altar behind the paper flowers,
So that Juan would come back to me,
And we could live again those lazy burning hours,
Forgetting the tap of my fan and my sharp words.
And I would only keep four of you,
Those two blue-white ones overhead,
To hang in my ears;
And those two orange ones yonder,
To fasten on my shoe buckles."

A little further along the street
A man sits stringing a brown guitar.
The smoke of his cigarette curls 'round his head,
And he too is humming, but other words:
"Think not that at your window I wait;
New love is better, the old is turned to hate.
Fate! Fate! All things pass away;
Life is forever, youth is for a day.
Love again if you may
Before the stars are blown out of the sky,
And the crickets die!
Babylon and Samarkand
Are mud walls in a waste of sand."

JOHN GOULD FLETCHER

THE HOT TAMALE MAN

Old Mexican tamale man,
You, trudging, come at twilight's lull
Tight-strapped upon your back a can
That holds your wares delectable:
        "Ta-ma-le, cal-i-en-te!"

Singsongy sweet, along the street,
Your cry brings all the children out,
And those who have a dime must greet
Your steps with an arresting shout:
        "Ten, please!" "And ten!" (*"Veinte!"*)

With smiling beam and knowing gleam,
You swing your load down to the curb
And lift the lid. Oh, savory steam
Imbued with chili pod and herb
And pepper hot, (*picante*)!

Shuck, sweet of sun, wraps well each one,
Ground, seasoned meat within a case
Of meal mush steamed till fully done—
Rare tidbit of a Southern race,
    Tamale, caliente!

A vendor old? Nay, I behold
A flash of senorita's eyes,
A dash of Indian bravery bold,
Moon-lyre, heart-fire,—romance that cries
    "Ta-ma-le, cal-i-en-te!"

HAZEL HARPER HARRIS

DESERT BORN

To-day who visits the desert sees
Alfalfa buds and poplar trees
And young wheat tall as a tall man's knees.

But I, who was born here, well I know
What makes a desert garden grow:

    Under the furrows the ground is wet—
    My mother's blood and my father's sweat!

Wheat-stalks, tell of my mother's fear,
Working the soil and my birth-date near:

Setting the point of her plow to the land,
The strength of her heart and the strength of her hand
Sown with her dreams in the treacherous sand.

Barley, green in the pastures, tell
Of the desert heat and the desert hell

My father fought in the sand and sun
Till the Dam was built and the Ditch was done
And river and laterals* flowed as one.

*The small ditches that carry water from the large canals directly onto the
land.

I, who was born here, well I know
What makes a desert garden grow:

Under the furrows the ground is wet—
My mother's blood and my father's sweat!

FAY M. YAUGER

NOON TRAIL

It was so still, that silence languished for a whisper.
It was so hot that pale flame cowered on the mesa.
A vulture, in the palsied blue above a lone foothill
Reposed upon its silken couch of ether, dozing.
And all the twisted desert people mutely smouldered,
        It was so hot—and still.

It was so clear that cities swam up out of nothing.
Tree-shadowed ponds of silvery, lilied whiteness, glistened.
The mountains, poppy-bosomed on the monstrous hem of
        distance,
Withdrew their filmy veils of finest-woven purple
And leaned their naked shoulders to the raptured
        canyons—
        It was so clear. So clear!

It was so grim, that danger tottered in its cavern.
It was so bleached, that whiteness groped its way, snow
        blinded.
Upon the pallid rock the lizards, flat and soundless,
Slid slowly eastward toward the promise of a shadow.
There was no place to kneel in all that shriveled vastness
        That was so white—and grim.

JENNIE HARRIS OLIVER

DESERT GODS

Cut deep by Time's inexorable hand,
These rocky cliffs lift massive shapes of red
And umber-brown above the canyon bed,
Where purple veils float low across a land
Of brooding mystery, of sun-bleached sand;
And scanty chaparral, sage brush and dead
Bunch-grass are after-banquet guests who tread
Deserted halls where bones of famine stand.

A vulture idly wheeling lone and high,
A lizard sunning on a gypsum ledge—
And palsied Time's irrevocable eye—
No other life is here to break the pledge
That Time will keep the desert unprofaned,
Wherein the static gods may walk unchained.

DAISY LEMON COLDIRON

DESERT HUNGER

Beneath rocks naked to the sky
    And old hills lean and brown,
Where carrion eagles circle by,
    Let me lie down.

I care not for the pastured plains
    Where long since I was born.
Give me dark hills with granite stains
    And rough with thorns.

There let me lie in death's own land
    Untroubled and alone
Till gnawing winds whet down the sand
    And strike a bone.

ARTHUR M. SAMPLEY

IN THE DESERT

There's no hiding here in the glare of the desert—
    If your coat is sham the sun shines through . . .
Here with the lovely things and the silence
    There is no crowd for saving you.

When hearts love here the love lasts longer,
    And hate here leaves a heavy scar.
But we, with the desert's beauty of distance,
    Are always dreaming of places far.

The tropic seas and the throb of cities,
    And harbors filled with the ships we knew.
We keep, with the sun and the stars and the silence,
    Life—and a promise glimmers through.

If you have come to start a kingdom—
    Our eyes looked on Rome and Tyre.
But if you come with dreams for baggage
    Sit with us by the cedar fire!

GLENN WARD DRESBACH

GHOST TOWN

Ghost town, dry husk of a city. Nameless.
Crumbling beneath the desert's brawling hand,
Its burst of poetry lived, its passions gone,
And only dry memories for a final stand.

Ghost town, that has no other life nor commerce
Than lizards; no sound of roulette wheel or gun;
Timbers seasoned to a mesquite thorn brittleness,
Sister to all towns fallen in the sun.

Ghost town, the plaything of the winds, or movie
Stars, who track the dust for local scene,
While rustlers, cowboys, hussies rise from Boothill
One with the echoing shadows on the screen.

EVERETT A. GILLIS

I AM DESERT-BORN

The cactus has its spike,
    The prickly-pear its spears;
I shall have the like,
    All of my years.

For I am desert-born—
    Stinging those who pass,
As the mesquite thorn,
    And the needle grass.

I am desert-born—
    And the desert marks its young,
With spike or spear or thorn,
    Or a sharp tongue.

VAIDA STEWART MONTGOMERY

IN THE DESERT

Three wolves crept out of the hills one night—
Skinny, and Sneaky, and old Cripple-toe:
Shadow-gray, shadow-black—slunk they all so,
Avoiding the trail of the full moonlight.
Skinny had puppies just able to see,

And Sneaky was last of a timber host.
Cripple was old as the hills—almost;
And all, were as famished as they could be.

A pinto limped on the dunes, alone.
Blinded and starving, he fumbled and fell.
And what was the end of his shuddering groan?
Night, and the silences, do not tell.

But Skinny, and Sneaky, and old Cripple-toe—
They fared as they fared: they know what they know.

JENNIE HARRIS OLIVER

IN A BORDER TOWN

Filth and mud welter in the crooked streets,
    Vice and misery behind closed doors,
An armless beggar's endless whine repeats
    His plea; he shows his putrid sores

To careless passersby who grin or swear
    In fluent Spanish, bidding him begone.
A slender girl with blue-black, lustrous hair,
    Slips from a door and softly hurries on;

She has a rendezvous, no doubt;
    Well, times are hard and one must live;
Through iron-bound windows sullen eyes peer out,
    From lives as sullen as the looks they give.

None but the wicked and the curious come here,
    Led by the glamor of an alien land,
Or the more sordid lure of girls and beer,
    Flinging their dollars with an easy hand.

This is the scum of half a continent,
    Gamblers and harpies and their silly prey,
On bestial pleasures or on money bent
    With all desire unleashed for one brief day.

Yet, on the wall beside each swinging door,
    The market place of drunkenness and shame,
The fading, crudely-lettered sign boards pour
    The liquid syllables of some proud name.

Names that were battle cries on that hot noon
    When the Moor fled on the Andalusian plain,
Names that were love songs beneath the Spanish moon,
    Or flew from pennons on the Spanish Main.

Names that are music when a minstrel sings
    Of half-forgotten battles lost and won,
Names that glitter like lost crowns of kings
    Or the bright heads of lances in the sun.

KENNETH C. KAUFMAN

LITTLE HOUSES

Little houses on quiet streets,
    Lawns and porches and garden swings,
Walls that listen as time repeats,
    A muffled sob, or the rustle of wings;
A cradle rocks while a mother sings,
    And the heart of a nation throbs and beats,
Simple and solid and homey things,
    Little houses on quiet streets.

Builders of bridges and men who dare
    Out of the side streets find their way,
Out in the wide world's glitter and glare,
    And the wide world listens to what they say.
Kingdoms totter, and nations sway,
    To the creak of an old time rocking chair
Where a mother watches a lad at play,
    A builder of bridges romping there.

Little houses where men grow great
    Measured by worth in a nation's need,
Lawn, and garden and picket gate,
    Have cradled men of a sturdy breed.
Flashing action and glowing deed,
    The hope of a nation to conquer fate,
Rests where the paths of a nation lead,
    In little houses where men grow great.

CAREY HOLBROOK

THERE IS SOMETHING ABOUT THE BRUSH

There is something about the brush that is like the dim of
    dawn,
    And the horses stomping, and the huisaches singing,
    The men saddling, and dim lights burning in the
    white jacales.
Mesquite and ebony, the lithe huajio casting its timid
    shade
    Enchanted and entattered and like finery—these
    calling,
    Come to my arroyos, Come to my valleys, Ride in the
    brake.
Reach on reach of the world's end, matted and whorled
    and brambly,

And the villages, hidden, the listless natives await,
And the slim vaqueros going about in forgotten tasks
Like the wind back and forth in the grass.
It is not strange that I should sing in other lands
(When great is my love, Maria!)
Of huisache trees and thy white hands,
And the road and dust to Randado.

JOHN HOUGHTON ALLEN

IF I HAD NEVER DREAMED OF POETRY

If I had never dreamed of poetry,
And been like my vaqueros and had had the very time,
I think, with all this bitter restlessness and this quick heart,
This haggard lack of chance, and this duteous love of song,
(If youth would wait, if beauty kept, if time itself had
          waited)
I'd have chucked the world and all to be a plain vaquero.

The old time, the violent days, the wind upon the acres . . .
Booted and spurred and poncho mantled, I would lie
          hidden
In some Sonoran hacienda like a bird of prey.
I should be quiet at noon in the shade of the patio.
Perhaps I would sing, or perhaps I'd not and never care,
And who can tell the greater loves I'd have than these,
Than the wispy songs, the ghosts, and the crumbled
          walls and all.

Our campfires greeting one unto the other all night
          long . . .
Till in the quick of morning and in the crying of dawn,
When the skinny steeds are saddled and coffee is ready,
The enchanted Sierra Madres gaunt and far in the desert,
The careless peons laughing that hold to a losing cause;

Captain, we are ready! Adventurers and knaves;
Who rallied Maximilian, who held the haunted empire,
Who never had a fatherland or ever held the odds,
Who never asked but for the dream, and the geese flying,
And a hand in the fall of powers and the open cause.
For we had had time to be hidalgos, later—if we cared,
To come home to the rancho some dim evening of winter,
When the brush is like the windblown garment of an
         Amazon,
To the old folks, and the narrow way, and the time to
         grow old in.

I should have time, then, to love quietly all these things
         about . . .
The ebony, the blue stone hills, the fern like huajio,
The fine horses, the courtesies, the Sunday fiestas.

To remember the distances under the blazing skies,
The song of spurs and the smell of dust and sage;
The breath of dawn, the flare of a match to a cigarette,
         lighting
Red and sienna faces, old rifles, silver bits, my compañeros.
To remember the wild roses, the giant joshua in bloom,
And our dusty file of fighting men in the yellow day.
To remember the night raid, the blow, the pillage,
The cantinas, the women as vivid as marihuana—
The skinny steeds, the yellow desert, the cavalry.

               JOHN HOUGHTON ALLEN

DEATH RODE A PINTO PONY

Death rode a pinto pony
    Along the Rio Grande,
Beside the trail his shadow
    Was riding on the sand.

The look upon his youthful face
    Was sinister and dark,
And the pistol in his scabbard
    Had never missed its mark.

The moonlight on the river
    Was bright as molten ore,
The ripples broke in whispers
    Along the sandy shore.

The breath of prairie flowers
    Had made the night-wind sweet,
And a mockingbird made merry
    In a lacy-leafed mesquite.

Death looked toward the river,
    He looked toward the land,
He took his broad sombrero off
    And held it in his hand,
And Death felt something touch him
    He could not understand.

The lights at Madden's ranch house
    Were brighter than the moon,
The girls came tripping in like deer,
    The fiddles were in tune,

And Death saw through the window
    The man he came to kill,
And he that did not hesitate
    Sat hesitating still.

A cloud came over the moon,
    The moon came out and smiled,
A coyote howled upon the hill,
    The mockingbird went wild.

Death drew his hand across his brow,
    As if to move a stain,
Then slowly turned his pinto horse
    And rode away again.

                WHITNEY MONTGOMERY

WHEN BILLY THE KID RIDES AGAIN

High are the mountains and low is the plain,
Where Billy the Kid comes a-ridin' again.

Old Juánico sees him—black on the moon,
And two haggard horsemen come following soon.

Now topping the rim-rock, now hid in a vale,
Four ghostly white riders press close on his trail.

No thudding of hoofbeats, no sound anywhere,
But nine silent dead men are racing the air.

Beyond the old courthouse and following fast,
The tenth pale pursuer springs out of the past.

Old Juánico sees them—no other eye can,
The galloping Kid and his strange caravan.

Fort Sumner to White Oaks, Tularosa to Bent—
Gaunt horsemen await him at each settlement.

For blood's in the moonmist, as two dozen dead
Swoop down the dim trails where their killer has fled.

Gray in the mountains and white on the plain,
At moon haunted midnight they're riding again.

Time shadows the silence in old Lincoln town—
Look! Billy the Kid comes a-galloping down!

S. OMAR BARKER

NEW MEXICO

I.

"What a God-forsaken desert!"
It was an eastern farmer, bred to the monotonous luxury of fat hogs and tall corn, that said it; and then I asked him if he knew
How the blue mountains would go walking with you
down
On the gray, gray road to Carrizozo town;
Or the young hill water would sing in the night,
Far up on the Pecos where the peaks are white.
And if he had seen, where the plains trails run,
Our tall phantom cities, born of the sun;
Or if he had known, as the black shawls know,
The gray sage paths of Chimayó.

II.

But yesterday I saw a lean-thonged man,
Sun-browned and strong, dig tough mesquite
To clear a virgin plot for planting corn,
Another breaking land for wheat:
Back-bent they were, yet singing in their eyes
I saw the soul-clear spirit of our skies.

It came to me again that we who love
Our *tierra encantada* here
Where cactus hills meet *vegas* lush and green
Could never hold her half so dear,
If she had been a coddling Mother, who,
For want of hardship lacked a spirit, too.

Oh, a sturdy town on a sand-blown plain
Is as brave as a ship on the storm-swept main!
And age-old mud on Ácoma's cliff
Is a nobler symbol than a hieroglyph.

In the tree-browned hills, so *muchachos* say,
Great wolves go talking their queer wild way;
And the brown boys know, down at Cochiti,
What the coyotes mean by their jubilee.

In the low green valleys when twilight comes
There's a sweet dim droning of forgotten drums.
Comes a phantom stage on the old town's streets
And in the cool plaza Spain's knighthood meets.

Do you know how the trees at the desert's rim
March out each night to a battle grim?
And the blue soldier-mountains walk with you as you go
Down the sand-gray roads of New Mexico?

S. OMAR BARKER

NEW MEXICO SPRING

I cannot say
Whether it swept westward
From the mountains
Where snowbanks linger still
Upon the crest,
Or whether it crept
Northward through the valley
That holds a turbid river
On its breast,
Or whether it came
Eastward on the desert
With murmurs from
A long forgotten sea,

Or whether it rose
Skyward; but from somewhere
The spring has come
Into the heart of me.

ETHEL B. CHENEY

OLD PLAZA IN ALBUQUERQUE

Beyond the brooding silence of the square
The Mission walls were dark against the faint
Dusk sky, and through a door I saw the flare
Of candle light on many a carven saint.

I saw a stately priest pace up and down,
Communing in the dark and narrow aisle;
I heard the whisper of his surpliced gown
Where worshippers have moved this long, long while.

A Spanish girl, wrapped in a shawl of lace,
Went to the altar-rail to kneel and pray;
The calm consuming beauty of her face
Was like a wind-fanned flame, too bright to stay.

I strolled away, as bells began to toll,
Across the plaza, all the silver sheen
Of stars shone through a giant tree whose bole
The fabled Coronado may have seen.

I left the square and I have not returned
To stand in silence as its lonely guest,
Yet night and day a somber flame has burned
Within my heart that does not let me rest.

And I would leave the noises of the town
To feel once more my tread on dreaming dust
That wears its weight of slumber like a crown—
I shall go back some day, I must, I must.

REID CROWELL

PEÑA BLANCA

For Thornton Wilder

Our Town is also folks and trees and houses,
A school and church, a graveyard on a hill
Where side by side lie old loam-married spouses
As they had living lain not quite so still.

But here all's naked earth. Cottonwoods suck
The bare earth-breast by walls and roofs of clay
Along dirt roads to sandy quilts that tuck
The dead in silt-screened beds. You hear them say:

"We are at home. To earthen walls our eyes
First opened, closed and opened night and morn,
And closed on them for good. Here each one lies
Like buried seed of cottonwood or corn,
Adobe-bred and born, re-wombed in earth,
To wait for what we dreamed, a greener birth."

FRAY ANGELICO CHAVEZ

CUNDIYO

As I came down from Cundiyo,
Upon the road to Chimayo
    I met three women walking;
Each held a sorrow to her breast,
And one of them a small cross pressed—
    Three black-shawled women walking.

'Now why is it that you must go
Up the long road to Cundiyo?'
    The old one did the talking:
'I go to bless a dying son.'
'And I a sweetheart never won.'
    Three women slowly walking.

The third one opened wide her shawl
And showed a new-born baby small
        That slept without a sorrow:
'And I, in haste that we be wed—
Too late, too late, if he be dead!
        The Padre comes tomorrow.'

As I went up to Cundiyo,
In the grey dawn from Chimayo,
        I met three women walking;
And over paths of sand and rocks
Were men who carried a long box—
Beside three women walking.

ALICE CORBIN

JUAN QUINTANA

The goat-herd follows his flock
Over the sandy plain,
And the goats nibble the rabbit-bush
Acrid with desert rain.

Old Juan Quintana's coat
Is a faded purple blue,
And his hat is a warm plum-brown,
And his trousers a tawny hue;

He is sunburnt like the hills,
And his eyes have a strange goat-look,
And when I came on him alone,
He suddenly quivered and shook.

Out in the hills all day,
The trees do funny things . . .
And a horse shaped like a man
Rose up from the ground on wings.

And a burro came and stood
With a cross, and preached to the flock,
While old Quintana sat
As cold as ice on a rock.

And sometimes the mountains move,
And the mesa turns about,
And Juan Quintana thinks he's lost
Till a neighbor hears him shout.

And they say with a little laugh
That he isn't quite right, up here;
And they'll have to get a *muchacho*
To help with the flock next year.

ALICE CORBIN

SHEEP HERDING

A gray, slow-moving, dust-bepowdered wave,
    That on the edges breaks to scattering spray,
Round which the faithful collies wheel and bark
    To scurry in the laggard feet that stray.
A babel of complaining tongues that make
    The dull air weary with their ceaseless fret;
Brown hills, akin to those of Galilee,
    On which the shepherds watch their charges yet.

The long, hot days; the stark, wind-beaten nights;
    No human presence, human sight or sound;
Grim, silent land of wasted hopes, where they
    Who came for gold oft times have madness found:
A bleating horror that fore-gathers speech;
    Freezing the word that from the lips would pass;
And sends the herdsman grovelling with his sheep,
    Face down and beast-like on the trampled grass.

.   .   .   .   .   .

The collies halt,—the slow herd sways and reels,
    Huddled in fear above a low ravine,
Where wild with fright a herd unshepherded
    Beats up and down—with something dark between:
A narrow circle that they will not cross;
    A thing to stop the maddest in their run—
A guarding dog, too weak to lift his head,
    Who licks a still hand shriveled in the sun.

SHARLOT M. HALL

THE TENT ROCKS

Jemez Mountains

What army pitched their tents upon this site?
What was the sin for which they turned to stone?
And did cold terror freeze each man alone
As he tossed restless in the waiting night?
Avid for glory in the morning's fight,
Sure that tomorrow's victory was their own—
By what strange power were they overthrown
To these fantastic pillars, salty-white?

Only the wind and lizards, stars and sun
Explore this sealed and solitary land
Of statue tents and statue banners furled.
And is this silenced camp the only one?
Or do they end at last as desert sand—
The camps of all the armies in the world?

ALLISON ROSS

TRUCHAS

Amigo, did you ever see Truchas?
Little town with trails unfurled,
Clutching the peak of a mountain,
Asleep on the rim of the world?

Did you ever see Truchas at dawn?
Its houses rising in light,
Like weary little sentinels,
From out the well of night?

Did you ever see Truchas at sunset?
When the bowl of earth below
Is filled to the brim with purple,
Spilled from the after-glow?

Did you ever see Truchas in moonlight?
A jagged silver frieze,
Against the top of the mountain,
On crumbling, silvered knees?—

Amigo, did you ever see Truchas?
With tired little roads running down;
The world at its feet as a foot-stool,
And a mountain peak for a crown?

FARONA KONOPAK

MORNING WALK—SANTA FE

In Burro Alley I saw no one
(This was hours before the sun),
Only the gray adobe walls
Leaning down like waterfalls,
Only the weedy patios,
No longer gay with strumming beaux.

Don Gaspar Street, processional,
Dipped and bowed; its shoulders tall
Were red with brick; gigantic words
Rose and soared thereon like birds.

The Alameda was a way
As tranquil as a field in May.
Under the cottonwoods it ran,
And under them I met a man
With frosty beard and cherry eyes.
He looked at me without surprise
Although I carried no pail of food
Nor drove a burro lashed with wood.

I met four burros on Cañon Road,
Every burro with his load;
I looked at them as anyone should,
Seeing a burro winged with wood.
Exactly as a river moves
Flowed the placid burro hooves.
I walked away from Cañon Road:
Mine had become a wingèd load.

The dawn was nearer than I knew;
The icy air came up like dew.
De Vargas Street was like a lane;
On Monte Sol I met the rain;
Dripping, he brought me home again.

LYNN RIGGS

THE SHAWLED MODEL

Pose demurely, Mexican maid,
A little ashamed of a model's trade,
Cast down your eyes and let your shawl
Darkly down your whole length fall,

Droop your mouth with sullenness,
Disconsolate with loveliness;
Let your spirit find a shade
Where you may look up unafraid.

PHILLIPS KLOSS

YELLOW

We drove out miles this afternoon
To see the yellow in the woods:
Mountain-sides of aspen.

And when the eye is tuned
To yellow and when autumn
Warms the very air with gold,
Who can see crimson or distant blues?
Each moment that I watched
A flock of magpies
Making a design,
Or glanced aside to note
An old rose window frame,
I saw instead
Chamisa, finger-tipped with saffron,
Or even sage, blooming to yellow,
Or dust, touched by the sun,
Or the road itself, unwinding itself;
And remembered that we had driven miles
To see the yellow in the woods.

Mountain-sides of aspen only?
There bloomed a daisy still
Against an adobe wall as yellow as the road;
Here a stubble-field where grain had ripened,
And under the shelter of a yellow hay-cock
A girl in a lemon-coloured dress.

Wheat before and during and after threshing;
Corn, leaning in the wind as fodder,
Drying on a wall as food,
Scattered on the ground as shucks:
Yellow, everything.
This stone, this parched hill,
This halo around the holy head
Of Jesus in an ancient church,
And the nimbus, glowing in the sun,
Around the tow-head of a boy.
Even the yellow glint of iris
In the eye of an old woman.

Yellow, reminder of fruit
Piled beneath canopies
In Mexican markets:
Bananas, limes, pitayas;
Reminder of sunsets and of stars,
Of moons, suns, planets and every straw
That ever broke a yellow desert camel's back.
Yellow of sunrise
Of jewelry, of pirate gold;
Yellow background of a painting of Salome,
Yellow parchment of an ancient tome
And a story written by O. Henry
On cheap, yellow copy-paper.

Yellow Chinese silk and Chinamen themselves.
Sallow skin of scholars in dark libraries;
Sunlight on the ocean, golden dreams,
And saffron cake made by Cornishmen
In California mining towns.

Yellow, chrome, cadmium, canary—
Synonyms, suggestions.
A novel by Aldous Huxley,
And one by Oppenheim;

The Yellow Book and sunflowers,
Kansas and yellow journals,
Honey, butter and yellow-jackets,
Canary cottage, cages and circus-wagons:
Whole worlds of flaming yellow fire—
And oblivion, yellow with the dust of ages!

. . . We drove out miles this afternoon
To see the yellow in the woods:
Mountain-sides of aspen.

WILLARD "SPUD" JOHNSON

THE AMERICAN EAGLE

The Dove of Liberty sat on an egg
And hatched another eagle.

But didn't disown the bird.

Down with all eagles! cooed the Dove.
And down all eagles began to flutter, reeling from their
        perches:
Eagles with two heads, Eagles with one, presently
        Eagles with none
Fell from the hooks and were dead.

Till the American Eagle was the only eagle left in the
        world.

Then it began to fidget, shifting from one leg to the other,
Trying to look like a pelican,
And plucking out of its plumage a few loose feathers
        to feather the nests of all
The new naked little republics come into the world.

But the feathers were, comparatively, a mere flea-bite.
And the bub-eagle that Liberty had hatched was growing
    a startling big bird
On the roof of the world;
A bit awkward, and with a funny squawk in his voice,
His mother Liberty trying always to teach him to coo
And him always ending with a yawp
Coo! Coo! Coo-ark! Coo-ark!
Quark!! Quark!!
YAWP!!!

So he clears his throat, the young Cock-eagle!

Now if the lilies of France lick Solomon in all his glory;
And the leopard cannot change his spots;
Nor the British lion his appetite;
Neither can a young Cock-eagle sit everlastingly
With an olive-sprig in his mouth.

It's not his nature.

The big bird of the Amerindian being the eagle,
Red men still stick themselves over with bits of his fluff,
And feel absolutely IT.

So better make up your mind, American Eagle,
Whether you're a sucking dove, *Roo-ooo-ooo!*
        Quark! Yawp!!
Or a pelican
Handing out a few loose golden breast-feathers, at
    moulting time;
Or a sort of prosperity-fowl
Fathering endless ten-dollar golden eggs,

Or whether it actually is an eagle you are,
With a Roman nose
And claws not made to shake hands with,
And a Me-Almighty eye.

The new full-fledged Republic
Chained to the perch of prosperity.
Overweening bird, full of screams of life, commanding a
    lucrative obedience.
Eagle of the Rockies, bird of men that are greedy,
Flapping your wings from your perch and commanding
    the greedy millions
Burrowing below you.
Opening great wings in the face of the sheep-faced ewe of
    the world
Who is losing her lamb;
Drinking a little blood, then spitting it out, young eagle,
    in distaste;
What bird are you, in the end?

What are you, American Eagle?
Will you feed for ever on the cold meat of prosperity?
Was your mother really a pelican, are you a strange cross?
Can you stay forever a tame half-breed cock on a golden
    perch?
Young eagle? Pelican-boy?

You're such a huge fowl!
And such a puzzler!

D. H. LAWRENCE

PART III   *Of Plains and Prairies*

To millions of movie-goers and readers of adventure tales the Southwest spells the open range, stampeding herds, shouting, singing, always gallant cowboys—the free life. Much of this concept, too, is reflected in the poetry of plains and prairie. In the years after the Civil War, partly to feed "Uncle Sam's Indians," the cattle industry developed on the grass lands of West Texas, Oklahoma, and New Mexico. Farmers and townsmen from the South and East and North learned to live without timber and with water always scarce and precious—of land and sky there was aplenty.

Around campfire, in bunk house, on lonely night herd, men sang the songs they knew back home, songs by Tom Moore and Bobby Burns or old folk ballads of British origin: "Barbara Allen," "Lord Thomas and Fair Ellinor," "The Ocean Burial." In ranch houses, when the work was all done in the fall, owners and cowboys swung their pardners and do-si-doed to these timeless tunes. Before long—just when or where, no one knows—"The Ocean Burial" became "The Dying Cowboy" and "My Bonnie Lies over the Ocean" became "The Cowboy's Dream." From the long drives of cattle to markets at Dodge City or Cheyenne new tunes and words sprang, as "Get Along, Little Dogies" and "Old Paint."

Before the end of the century Howard Thorp and John Lomax began independent collections of cowboy ballads (Thorp even wrote a few) and gradually educated scholars and publishers to the value of these songs of the range. The phonograph, radio, movie, and television have brought them to all the world.

After 1870 the local color movement in American literature found expression in the verses of Bret Harte, Joaquin Miller, and others. Later Rudyard Kipling and Robert W. Service affected American poetry. In the Southwest these influences merged with the cowboy ballad tradition to produce many spirited, story telling, hero-creating, often humorous poems. Joaquin Miller's rhetorical "Kit Carson's Ride," published in 1871, was followed by Frank Desprez's "Lasca," swift moving, hard riding poems of prairie fires and stampeding herds.

Larry Chittenden's *Ranch Verses* (1893) ran through many editions. His best known poem "The Cowboy's Christmas Ball" has brought fame to the little town of Anson, Texas, where thousands gather each year to re-dance in pioneer costume the famous ball of 1885. Larry Chittenden—a New York journalist turned ranchman—rather self-consciously employed ungrammatical Western dialect for the cowboys of his poems. Early in the twentieth century Arthur Chapman, another Eastern journalist, came to the Southwest and likewise wrote of the land and the people in the Bret Harte manner. The title of his best known poem "Out Where the West Begins" has become trite on the folk tongue. It supplies a large city newspaper, the *Fort Worth Star-Telegram,* with the descriptive phrase in its masthead.

Eugene Manlove Rhodes, coming to New Mexico in 1881, ranched, wrote novels, and an occasional poem. Incensed by a newspaper quip, he defended the cowboy, his courage and hardships endured, in the ironical "Hired Man on Horseback." Gene Rhodes' stories and poems came straight from the life he lived, and he found it a good life though a hard one.

In more recent years Henry Herbert Knibbs, Badger Clark, and S. Omar Barker have written of plains and cowpunchers with psychological insight and broad humor. Knibbs' "Old Bill" is a laconic character sketch as authentic as a Peter Hurd portrait. Badger Clark's High-Chin Bob is blood brother to Pecos Bill of tall-tale fame. S. Omar Barker's "Jack Potter's Courting," like a well told anecdote, saves the punch for the last line. All three poets are professional writers and skilled craftsmen.

When the open range gave way to barbed wire, cattle raising and marketing became less of a high adventure and more of a calculated business. Cities and spreading towns grew on the plains. Howard Thorp lived to inquire sadly, "What has become of the punchers?" E. E. Dale and Kenneth Kaufman wrote nostalgically of the prairie wagons and passing herds of their boyhoods. Violet Mc-Dougal saw a "phantom round-up" in the "ghostly light" over her sleeping city.

Although the ballad-like narrative is the characteristic verse form of the range, many fine emotional and descriptive lyrics have been written of the open spaces: Karle Wilson Baker's "Song of the Forerunners," George Bond's "Sketches of the Texas Prairie," Berta Hart Nance's "Cattle," Stanley Vestal's "Prairie Pictographs," to name a few. Two of the most haunting are Margaret Bell Houston's "Song from Traffic" and John McClure's "In Bourbon Street," each poet voicing from far away cities a longing for his plains and prairies when spring is in the air. Of the harshness and violence of the Southwest a few realists have written, as Vera Holding in "Sand Storm" and "Tornado"; but this is a minor note in a body of poetry that is dominantly optimistic and youthful in spirit.

A HOME ON THE RANGE

Oh, give me a home where the buffalo roam,
Where the deer and the antelope play,
Where seldom is heard a discouraging word
And the skies are not cloudy all day.

Home, home on the range,
Where the deer and the antelope play;
Where seldom is heard a discouraging word
And the skies are not cloudy all day.

Where the air is so pure, the zephyrs so free,
The breezes so balmy and light,
That I would not exchange my home on the range
For all of the cities so bright.

The red man was pressed from this part of the West,
He's likely no more to return
To the banks of Red River where seldom if ever
Their flickering camp-fires burn.

How often at night when the heavens are bright
With the light from the glittering stars,
Have I stood here amazed and asked as I gazed
If their glory exceeds that of ours.

Oh, I love these wild flowers in this dear land of ours,
The curlew I love to hear scream,
And I love the white rocks and the antelope flocks
That graze on the mountain-tops green.

Oh, give me a land where the bright diamond sand
Flows leisurely down the stream;
Where the graceful white swan goes gliding along
Like a maid in a heavenly dream.

Then I would not exchange my home on the range,
Where the deer and the antelope play;
Where seldom is heard a discouraging word
And the skies are not cloudy all day.

Home, home on the range,
Where the deer and the antelope play;
Where seldom is heard a discouraging word
And the skies are not cloudy all day.

JOHN A LOMAX, Collector

OLD PAINT

Refrain:
Good-bye, Old Paint, I'm a-leavin' Cheyenne.
Good-bye, Old Paint, I'm a-leavin' Cheyenne.

My foot in the stirrup, my pony won't stand;
Good-bye, Old Paint, I'm a-leavin' Cheyenne.

I'm a-leavin' Cheyenne, I'm off for Montan';
Good-bye, Old Paint, I'm a-leavin' Cheyenne.

I'm a-ridin' Old Paint, I'm a-leadin' Old Fan;
Good-bye, Old Paint, I'm a-leavin' Cheyenne.

With my feet in the stirrups, my bridle in my hand;
Good-bye, little Annie, I'm off for Cheyenne.

Old Paint's a good pony, he paces when he can;
Good-bye, little Annie, I'm off for Cheyenne.

Oh hitch up your horses and feed 'em some hay,
And seat yourself by me so long as you stay.

My horses ain't hungry, they'll not eat your hay;
My wagon is loaded and rolling away.

My foot in my stirrup, my reins in my hand;
Good-morning, young lady, my horses won't stand.

Good-bye, Old Paint, I'm a-leavin' Cheyenne,
Good-bye, Old Paint, I'm a-leavin' Cheyenne.

N. HOWARD "JACK" THORP, Collector

THE DYING COWBOY

"Oh, bury me not on the lone prairie";
Those words came slow and mournfully
From the pallid lips of a youth that lay
On his dying couch at the close of day.

He had wasted and pined till o'er his brow
Death's shadows fast were drawing now;
He had thought of home and the loved ones nigh,
As the cowboys gathered to see him die.

How oft have I listened to those well-known words,
The wild wind and the sound of birds;
He had thought of home and the cottonwood boughs,
Of the scenes that he loved in his childhood hours.

"I have always wished to be laid, when I died,
In the old churchyard on the green hillside,
By the grave of my father, oh, let my grave be;
Oh, bury me not on the lone prairie.

"I wish to be laid where a mother's care
And a sister's tear can mingle there;
Where friends can come and weep o'er me;
Oh, bury me not on the lone prairie.

"Oh, bury me not—" and his voice failed there;
They paid no heed to his dying prayer;
In a narrow grave just six by three,
They laid him there on the lone prairie.

Where the dewdrops fall and the butterfly rests,
The wild rose blooms on the prairie's crest,
Where the coyotes howl and the wind sports free,
They laid him there on the lone prairie.

N. HOWARD "JACK" THORP, Collector

GET ALONG, LITTLE DOGIES

As I walked out one morning for pleasure,
I spied a cow-puncher all riding alone;
His hat throwed back and his spurs was a-jinglin'
As he approached me a-singin' this song:

Whoopee ti yi yo, git along, little dogies,
It's your misfortune, and none of my own.
Whoopee ti yi yo, git along, little dogies,
For you know Wyoming will be your new home.

Early in the spring we round up the dogies,
Mark and brand and bob off their tails;
Round up our horses, load up the chuck-wagon,
Then throw the dogies upon the North trail.

It's whoopin' and yellin' and drivin' the dogies;
Oh, how I wish you would go on;
It's whoopin' and punchin', go on, little dogies,
For you know Wyoming will be your new home.

Some boys go up the trail for pleasure,
But that's where you get it most awfully wrong;
For you haven't an idea the trouble they give us
While we go drivin' them all along.

Your mother she was raised 'way down in Texas,
Where the jimson weed and sand-burrs grow;
Now we'll fill you up on prickly pear and cholla,
Till you are ready for the trail to Idaho.

Oh, you'll be soup for Uncle Sam's Injuns;
"It's beef, heap beef," I hear them cry.
Git along, git along, little dogies,
You're goin' to be beef steers by and by.

N. HOWARD "JACK" THORP, Collector

LITTLE JOE, THE WRANGLER

Little Joe, the wrangler, will never wrangle more;
    His days with the "remuda"—they are done.
'Twas a year ago last April he joined the outfit here,
    A little "Texas stray'" and all alone.

'Twas long late in the evening he rode up to the herd
    On a little old brown pony he called Chow;
With his brogan shoes and overalls a harder-looking kid,
    You never in your life had seen before.

His saddle 'twas a Southern kack built many years ago,
    An O. K. spur on one foot idly hung,
While his "hot roll" in a cotton sack was loosely tied
        behind
    And a canteen from the saddle horn he'd slung.

He said he had to leave his home, his daddy'd married
        twice,
    And his new ma beat him every day or two;
So he saddled up old Chow one night and "lit a shuck"
        this way—
    Thought he'd try and paddle now his own canoe.

Said he'd try and do the best he could if we'd only give
        him work,
    Though he didn't know "straight" up about a cow;
So the boss he cut him out a mount and kinder put him on,
    For he sorter liked the little stray somehow.

Taught him how to herd the horses and learn to know
        them all,
    To round 'em up by daylight; if he could
To follow the chuck-wagon and to always hitch the team
    And help the "cosinero" rustle wood.

We'd driven to Red River and the weather had been fine;
    We were camped down on the south side in a bend,
When a norther commenced blowing and we doubled
        up our guards,
    For it took all hands to hold the cattle then.

Little Joe, the wrangler, was called out with the rest,
    And scarcely had the kid got to the herd,
When the cattle they stampeded; like a hailstorm, long
        they flew,
    And all of us were riding for the lead.

'Tween the streaks of lightning we could see a horse far
        out ahead—
    'Twas little Joe, the wrangler, in the lead;
He was riding "Old Blue Rocket" with his slicker 'bove
        his head,
    Trying to check the leaders in their speed.

At last we got them milling and kinder quieted down,
    And the extra guard back to the camp did go;
But one of them was missin', and we all knew at a glance
    'Twas our little Texas stray—poor Wrangler Joe.

Next morning just at sunup we found where Rocket fell,
    Down in a washout twenty feet below;
Beneath his horse, mashed to a pulp, his spurs had rung
        the knell
    For our little Texas stray—poor Wrangler Joe.

                N. HOWARD "JACK" THORP

THE COWBOYS' CHRISTMAS BALL

To *The Ranchmen of Texas*

'Way out in Western Texas, where the Clear Fork's
      waters flow,
Where the cattle are "a-browzin'," an' the Spanish ponies
      grow;
Where the Northers "come a-whistlin' " from beyond
      the neutral strip;
And the prairie dogs are sneezin', as if they had "The
      Grip";
Where the coyotes come a-howlin' 'round the ranches after
      dark,
And the mocking-birds are singin' to the lovely "medder
      lark";
Where the 'possum and the badger, and rattle-snakes
      abound,
And the monstrous stars are winkin' o'er a wilderness
      profound;
Where lonesome, tawny prairies melt into airy streams,
While the Double Mountains slumber, in heavenly kinds
      of dreams;
Where the antelope is grazin' and the lonely plovers call—
It was there that I attended "The Cowboys' Christmas
      Ball."

The town was Anson City, old Jones's county seat,
Where they raise Polled Angus cattle, and waving
      whiskered wheat;
Where the air is soft and "bammy," an' dry an' full of
      health,
And the prairies is explodin' with agricultural wealth;
Where they print the *Texas Western,* that Hec. McCann
      supplies,
With news and yarns and stories, uv most amazin' size;

Where Frank Smith "pulls the badger," on knowin'
        tenderfeet,
And Democracy's triumphant, and mighty hard to beat;
Where lives that good old hunter, John Milsap from
        Lamar,
Who "used to be the Sheriff, back East, in Paris, sah!"
'Twas there, I say, at Anson, with the lively "widder
        Wall,"
That I went to that reception, "The Cowboys' Christmas
        Ball."

The boys had left the ranches and come to town in piles;
The ladies—"kinder scatterin' "—had gathered in for
        miles.
And yet the place was crowded, as I remember well,
'Twas got for the occasion, at "The Morning Star Hotel."
The music was a fiddle an' a lively tambourine,
And a "viol came imported," by the stage from Abilene.
The room was togged out gorgeous—with mistletoe and
        shawls,
And candles flickered frescoes, around the airy walls.
The "wimmin folks" looked lovely—the boys looked
        kinder treed,
Till their leader commenced yellin': "Whoa! fellers, let's
        stampede,"
And the music started sighin', an' awailin' through the
        hall,
As a kind of introduction to "The Cowboys' Christmas
        Ball."

The leader was a feller that came from Swenson's Ranch,
They called him "Windy Billy," from "little Deadman's
        Branch."
His rig was "kinder keerless," big spurs and high-heeled
        boots;
He had the reputation that comes when "fellers shoots."
His voice was like a bugle upon the mountain's height;
His feet were animated, an' a *mighty, movin' sight,*

When he commenced to holler, "Neow fellers, stake yer
        pen!
"Lock horns ter all them heifers, an' russle 'em like men.
"Saloot yer lovely critters; neow swing an' let 'em go,
"Climb the grape vine 'round 'em—all hands do-ce-do!
"You Mavericks, jine the round-up—Jest skip her
        waterfall,"
Huh! hit wuz gettin' happy, "The Cowboys' Christmas
        Ball!"

The boys were tolerable skittish, the ladies powerful neat,
That old bass viol's music *just got there with both feet!*
That wailin', frisky fiddle, I never shall forget;
And Windy kept a singin'—I think I hear him yet—
"O Xes, chase your squirrels, an' cut 'em to one side,
"Spur Treadwell to the center, with Cross P Charley's
        bride,
"Doc. Hollis down the middle, an' twine the ladies' chain,
"Varn Andrews pen the fillies in big T Diamond's train.
"All pull yer freight tergether, neow swallow fork an'
        change,
" 'Big Boston' lead the trail herd, through little
        Pitchfork's range.
"Purr 'round yer gentle pussies, neow rope 'em! Balance
        all!"
Huh! hit wuz gettin' active—"The Cowboys' Christmas
        Ball!"

The dust riz fast an' furious, we all just galloped 'round,
Till the scenery got so giddy, that Z Bar Dick was downed.
We buckled to our partners, an told 'em to hold on,
Then shook our hoofs like lightning, until the early
        dawn.
Don't tell me 'bout cotillions, or germans. No sir 'ee!
That whirl at Anson City just takes the cake with me.
I'm sick of lazy shufflin's, of them I've had my fill,
Give me a frontier break-down, backed up by Windy Bill.
McAllister ain't nowhar! when Windy leads the show,

I've seen 'em both in harness, and so I sorter know—
Oh, Bill, I shan't forget yer, and I'll oftentimes recall
That lively gaited sworray—"The Cowboys' Christmas
    Ball."

WILLIAM LAWRENCE "LARRY" CHITTENDEN

LASCA

I want free life, and I want fresh air;
And I sigh for the canter after the cattle,
The crack of the whips like shots in a battle,
The mellay of horns and hoofs and heads
That wars and wrangles and scatters and spreads;
The green beneath and the blue above,
The dash and danger, and life and love.
And Lasca!
    Lasca used to ride
On a mouse-gray mustang close to my side,
With blue *serape* and bright-belled spur;
I laughed with joy as I looked at her.
Little knew she of books or of creeds;
An *Ave Maria* sufficed her needs;
Little she cared, save to be by my side,
To ride with me, and ever to ride,
From San Saba's shore to Lavaca's tide.

She was as bold as the billows that beat,
She was as wild as the breezes that blow;
From her little head to her little feet
She was swayed in her suppleness to and fro
By each gust of passion; a sapling pine,
That grows on the edge of a Kansas bluff,
And wars with the wind when the weather is rough,
Is like this Lasca, this love of mine.
She would hunger that I might eat,

Would take the bitter and leave the sweet;
But once, when I made her jealous for fun,
At something I'd whispered, or looked, or done,
One Sunday in San Antonio,
To a glorious girl on the Alamo,
She drew from her garter a dear little dagger,
And—sting of a wasp!—it made me stagger!
An inch to the left, or an inch to the right,
And I shouldn't be maundering here to-night;
But she sobbed, and, sobbing, so swiftly bound
Her torn *rebosa* about the wound,
That I quite forgave her. Scratches don't count
    In Texas, down by the Rio Grande.

Her eye was brown—a deep, deep brown—
Her hair was darker than her eye;
And something in her smile and frown,
Curled crimson lip and instep high,
Showed that there ran in each blue vein,
Mixed with the milder Aztec strain,
The vigorous vintage of old Spain.
She was alive in every limb
With feeling, to the finger-tips;
And when the sun is like a fire,
And sky one shining, soft sapphire,
One does not drink in little sips.
    *   *   *   *   *

The air was heavy, the night was hot,
I sat by her side, and forgot—forgot
The herd that were taking their rest,
Forgot that the air was close oppressed,
That the Texas norther comes sudden and soon,
In the dead of the night, or the blaze of the noon—
That once let the herd at its breath take fright,
Nothing on earth can stop its flight;
And woe to the rider, and woe to the steed,
Who falls in front of their mad stampede!
    *   *   *   *   *

Was that thunder? I grasped the cord
Of my swift mustang without a word.
I sprang to the saddle, and she clung behind.
Away! on a hot chase down the wind!
But never was fox-hunt half so hard.
And never was steed so little spared;
For we rode for our lives. You shall hear how we fared
    In Texas, down by the Rio Grande.

The mustang flew, and we urged him on;
There was one chance left, and you have but one.
Halt! jump to the ground, and shoot your horse;
Crouch under his carcass, and take your chance;
And if the steers in their frantic course
Don't batter you both to pieces at once,
You may thank your star; if not, good-bye
To the quickening kiss and the long-drawn sigh,
And the open air and the open sky,
    In Texas, down by the Rio Grande!

The cattle gained on us, and, just as I felt
For my old six-shooter behind in my belt,
Down came the mustang, and down came we,
Clinging together, and—what was the rest?
A body that spread itself on my breast,
Two arms that shielded my dizzy head,
Two lips that hard on my lips were pressed;
Then came thunder in my ears,
As over us surged the sea of steers,
Blows that beat blood into my eyes;
And when I could rise—
Lasca was dead!
      *   *   *   *   *

I gouged out a grave a few feet deep,
And there in Earth's arms I laid her to sleep;
And there she is lying, and no one knows,
And the summer shines and the winter snows;
For many a day the flowers have spread
A pall of petals over her head;
And the little gray hawk hangs aloft in the air,

And the sly coyote trots here and there,
And the black snake glides and glitters and slides
Into a rift in a cotton-wood tree;
And the buzzard sails on,
And comes and is gone,
Stately and still like a ship at sea;
And I wonder why I do not care
For the things that are like the things that were.
Does my heart lie buried there
    In Texas, down by the Rio Grande?

                            FRANK DESPREZ

THE HIRED MAN ON HORSEBACK

(With apologies to G. K. Chesterton and Don Juan
of Austria)

The typical cowboy is . . . simply a riding farmhand.—
James Stephens; *International Book Review*

The cowboy, after all, was never anything more than a
hired man on horseback.—Editorial Page; *Minneapolis
Tribune, San Francisco Chronicle*

Harp and flute and violin, throbbing through the night,
Merry eyes and tender eyes, dark head and bright;
Moon shadow on the sun dial to mark the moments fleet,
The magic and enchanted hours where moonlight lovers
        meet;
And the harp notes come all brokenly by night winds
        stirred—
But the hired man on horseback is singing to the herd!
    (Whoopie-ti-yo-o-o! Hi yo-o, my little dogies!)
    Doggerel upon his lips and valor in his heart,
    Not to flinch and not to fail, not to shirk his part;
    Wearily and wearily he sees the stars wheel by,
    And he knows his guard is nearly done by the great
        clock in the sky.

He hears the Last Guard coming and he hears their
     song begun,
A foolish song he will forget when he forgets the sun.
(*Whoopie ti yo-o-o! Hi yo-o, my little dogies!*)
'We got 'em now, you sleepy men, so pull your
     freight to bed
And pound your ear an hour or two before the east is
     red.'

If to his dreams a face may come? Ah, turn your eyes
     away,
Nor guess that face may come by dream that never
     comes by day.
Red dawn breaking through the desert murk;
The hired man on horseback goes laughing to his
     work.

The broker's in his office before the stroke of ten,
He buys and smiles and he sells and smiles at the word of
     other men;
But he gets his little commission flat, whether they buy or
     sell,
So be it drouth or storm or flood, the broker's crops do well.
They are short of Katy Common, they are long on Zinc
     Preferred—
But the hired man on horseback is swimming with the
     herd!
    White horns gleaming where the flood rolls brown,
    Lefty fighting the lower point as the current sweeps
       them down,
    Lefty fighting the stubborn steers that will not turn
       or slow,
    They press beside him, they swim below him—'Come
       out and let them go!'
    But Lefty does not leave them and Lefty tries once
       more,
    He is swinging the wild leaders in toward the north-
       ern shore;
    'He'll do to ride the river with!' (Bridging the years
       between,

Men shall use those words again—and wonder what
    they mean.)
He is back to turn the stragglers in to follow the
    leaders through,
When a cottonwood snag comes twisting down and
    cuts the herd in two;
When a whirling snag comes twisting down with
    long arms lashing hate,
On wearied horse and wearied man—and they see it
    come, too late!
—A brown hand lifted in the splashing spray;
Sun upon a golden head that never will be gray;
A low mound bare until new grass is grown—
But the Palo Pinto trail herd has crossed the
    Cimarron!

A little midnight supper when the play is done,
Glancing lights and sparkling cycs—the night is just
    begun.
Beauteous night, O night of love!—Youth and joy are met.
Shine on our enchantment still! 'Sweet, your eyes are wet.'
'Dear, they sing for us alone!' Such the lover's creed.
—But the hired man on horseback is off with the
    stampede!

    There is no star in the pit-dark night, there is none
        to know or blame,
    And a hundred yards to left or right, there is safety
        there—and shame!
    A stone throw out on either side, with none to guess
        or tell—
    But the hired man on horseback has raised the
        rebel yell!
    He has turned to loosen his saddle strings, he has
        fumbled his slicker free,
    He whirls it high and he snaps it wide wherever the
        foremost be,
    He slaps it onto a longhorn's eyes till he falters in
        his stride—

An oath and a shot, a laugh and a shot, and his wild
      mates race beside;
A pony stumbles—no, he is up, unhurt and
      running still;
'Turn 'em, turn 'em, turn 'em, Charlie!
      Good boy, Bill!'
They are crashing through the cactus flats where the
      badger holes are thick;
Day is breaking, clouds are lifting, leaders turn to
      mill—
'Hold 'em, cowboys! Turn 'em, Charlie!—God!
      Where's Bill!'

The proud Young Intellectuals, a cultured folk are these,
They scorn the lowly Babbitts and their hearts are
      overseas;
They turn their backs upon us, and if we ask them why
They smile like jesting Pilate, and they stay for no reply;
They smile at faith and honor, and they smile at shame
      and crime—
But the old Palo Pinto man is calling for his time.
      For he heard old voices and he heard hoofs beat,
      Songs that long ago were gay to time with drumming
            feet;
      Bent back straightens and dim eyes grow bright—
      The last man on horseback rides on into the night!
Cossack and Saracen
Shout their wild welcome then,
Ragged proud Conquistadores claim him kind and
      kin,
And the wild Beggars of the Sea leap up to swell
      the din:
And Hector leans upon the wall, and David bends to
      scan
This new brown comrade for the old brown clan,
The great hearted gentlemen who guard the outer
      wall
Black with sin and stained with blood— and faithful
      through it all;

Still wearing for all ornament the scars they won
    below—
And the Lord God of Out-of-Doors, He cannot let
    them go!
They have halted the hired horseman beyond the
    outer gate,
But the gentlemen adventurers cry shame that he
    should wait;
And the sour saints soften, with a puzzled grin,
As Esau and Ishmael press to let their brother in.
Hat tip-tilted and his head held high,
Brave spurs jingling as he passes by—
Gray hair tousled and his lips a-quirk—
'To the Master of the Workmen, with the tally of
    his work!'

                    EUGENE MANLOVE RHODES

THE GLORY TRAIL

High-Chin Bob

'Way high up the Mogollons,
    Among the mountain tops,
A lion cleaned a yearlin's bones
    And licked his thankful chops,
When on the picture who should ride,
    A-trippin' down a slope,
But High-Chin Bob, with sinful pride
    And mav'rick hungry rope.

"Oh, glory be to me," says he,
    "And fame's unfadin' flowers!
All meddlin' hands are far away;
I ride my good top-hawse today
And I'm top-rope of the Lazy J—
    "Hi! kitty cat, you're ours!"

103

That lion licked his paw so brown
       And dreamed soft dreams of veal—
And then the circlin' loop sung down
       And roped him 'round his meal.
He yowled quick fury to the world
       Till all the hills yelled back;
The top hawse gave a snort and whirled
       And Bob caught up the slack.
       "Oh, glory be to me," laughs he.
              "We hit the glory trail.
       No human man as I have read
       Darst loop a ragin' lion's head,
       Nor ever hawse could drag one dead
       Until we told the tale."

'Way high up the Mogollons
       That top-hawse done his best,
Through whippin' brush and rattlin' stones,
       From canyon-floor to crest.
But ever when Bob turned and hoped
       A limp remains to find,
A red-eyed lion, belly roped
       But healthy, loped behind.
       "Oh, glory be to me," grunts he.
              "This glory trail is rough,
       Yet even till the Judgment Morn
       I'll keep this dally 'round the horn,
       For never any hero born
              Could stoop to holler: 'Nuff!'"

Three suns had rode their circle home
       Beyond the desert's rim,
And turned their star-herds loose to roam
       The ranges high and dim;
Yet up and down and 'round and 'cross
       Bob pounded, weak and wan,
For pride still glued him to his hawse
       And glory drove him on.
       "Oh, glory be to me," sighs he.

"He kain't be drug to death,
But now I know beyond a doubt
Them heroes I have read about
Was only fools that stuck it out
To end of mortal breath."

'Way high up the Mogollons
    A prospect man did swear
That moon dreams melted down his bones
    And hoisted up his hair:
A ribby cow-hawse thundered by,
    A lion trailed along,
A rider, ga'nt but chin on high,
    Yelled out a crazy song.

"Oh, glory be to me!" cries he,
    "And to my noble noose!
Oh, stranger, tell my pards below
I took a rampin' dream in tow,
And if I never lay him low,
    I'll never turn him loose!"

BADGER CLARK

OLD BILL

Young Sam went broke and hoofed it out of town,
When, on the mesa trail, came riding down
His partners of the range, a cowboy crew,
Rough-witted, ready-fisted, tough and true,
But bound to have their joke—and Sam was it,
And didn't like their talk a little bit.

"How, Sam? You took to walkin' for your health?
Or mebby-so you're lookin' for yore wealth,
Prospectin' like, and gazin' at the ground;
Good-luck, old-timer—when you git it found!"

Another puncher turned as he rode by
And made a show of dealing, low and high,
But never said a word—while Sam, he cussed
And watched his outfit kicking up the dust.

Sam wished he had some dust safe in his kick.
Last night he'd spread his wages pretty thick
In town—and he'd seemed to overlook.
A gambler from The Dalles promptly took,
Even to young Sam's outfit, horse and gun,
Then Sammy quit because his dough was done.

Yet, as that cavalcade of punchers passed,
Old Bill, the foreman, and the very last
To pose as a Samaritan, came by,
A sort of evening twinkle in his eye,
Pulled up and told the youngster what he thought
About the easy way that he'd been caught:
Called him more names, with adjectives between,
Than ever had been either heard or seen
Till then—then slowly finished, "which, my son,
Was comin' to you. Now you've had yore fun,
Take this here lead-rope."
                    Sam he mouched across:
"I see you done that gambler for my hoss."
Bill nodded—once—and slowly rolled a smoke:
"Yes. That there Dalles gent would have his joke;
He run five aces on your Uncle Bill,
But he ain't runnin' now. He's keepin' still."

Sam gazed at Bill with wide, astonished eye;
"You plugged him!" Bill just gazed across the sky
And pulled the flop of his old Stetson hat.
"Well, son, there's some alive would call it that.
Jest fork your hoss, set straight, don't bow yore head,
Or tell the boys a gosh-durned word I said.
Come on! *Yo're* livin' yet, and you are young;
But you'll be older, next time you git stung."

Bill drew his gun—poked out an empty shell,
And Sam rode thoughtful-like, for quite a spell.

HENRY HERBERT KNIBBS

THE LAST DRIFT

I've sold the old ranch, stock and all,
    And let my cowboys go;
I'm driftin' into town this fall,
    'Long with the first deep snow;
I've stuck it out, the last cowman
    'Twixt here and Painted Stone;
For forty years—a healthy span—
    I've fought my fight alone.

I've fought the northers and the sheep,
    I've won, and lost, and won;
But every year, at spring's first peep,
    The old chuck wagon'd run;
Now it has vanished, with the rest——
    Its round-up days are o'er—
The range is gone—I s'pose it's best—
    And fate has closed the score.

Last night I dreamed of olden days,
    When cattle roamed the hills
And cowboys rode the prairie ways—
    No more their presence thrills——
I saw the moon shine through a rift,
    On him who stood night guard,
But woke to find that I must drift,
    Though driftin's hard, plumb hard!

ARTHUR CHAPMAN

JACK POTTER'S COURTIN'

Now young Jack Potter was a man who knowed the ways
        of steers,
From burr-nests in their hairy tails to the ticks inside
        their ears.
A Texian and cowhand, to the saddle born and bred,
He could count a trail herd on the move and never miss
        a head.
But one day on a tally, back in eighteen eighty-four,
He got to actin' dreamy, and he sure did miss the score.
The Old Man knowed the symptoms: "Jack, you ain't no
        good like this.
I'll give you just ten days to go and find out what's amiss."
"A miss" was just what ailed him, for he'd fell in love
        and stuck,
With sweet Miss Cordie Eddy, fresh from Louisville,
        Kentuck.
So now Jack rode a hundred miles a-sweatin' with the
        thought
Of sweetsome words to ask her with, the way a feller
        ought:
"I'm just a humble cowhand, Miss Cordie, if you please,
That hereby asks your heart an' hand upon my bended
        knees!"
It sounded mighty simple, thus rehearsed upon the trail,
But when he come to Cordie's house, his words all seemed
        to fail.
'Twas "Howdy, ma'am!" and "how's the crops?" and
        "how's your Pa an' Ma?"
For when it come to askin her, he couldn't come to taw.
He took her to a dance one night. The hoss she rode was
        his.
"He's a dandy little horse," she says, and "Yep," says
        Jack, "he is."
They rode home late together and the moon was ridin' high,
And Jack, he got to talkin' 'bout the stars up in the sky,
And how they'd guide a trail herd like they do sea goin'
        ships—

But words of love and marriage, they just wouldn't pass
         his lips.
So he spoke about the pony she was ridin', and he said:
"You'll note he's fancy gaited an' don't never fight his
         head."
"He's sure a little dandy," she agrees and heaves a sigh.
Jack says: "Why you can have him—that is, maybe—
         when I die!"
He figgered she might savvy what he meant, or maybe
         guess,
And give him that sweet answer which he hoped for,
         namely "yes."
But when they reached the ranch house he was still
         a-wonderin' how
He would ever pop the question—and he had to do it now
Or wait and sweat and suffer till the drive was done that
         fall,
When maybe she'd be married, and he'd lose her after all.
He put away her saddle, led his pony to the gate:
"I reckon I'll be driftin', ma'am. It's gittin' kinder late."
Her eyes was bright as starlight and her lips looked sweet
         as flowers. . . .
Says Jack: "Now this here pony—is he mine—or is he
         ours?"
"Our pony, Jack!" she answered, and her voice was soft
         as moss.
Then Jack, he *claims* he kissed her—but she claims he
         kissed the hoss!

                                S. OMAR BARKER

WHAT'S BECOME OF THE PUNCHERS?

      What's become of the punchers
      We rode with long ago?
      The hundreds and hundreds of cowboys
      We all of us used to know?

Sure, some were killed by lightning,
Some when the cattle run,
Others were killed by horses,
And some with the old six-gun.

Those who worked on the round-up,
Those of the branding-pen,
Those who went out on the long trail drive
And never returned again.

We know of some who have prospered,
We hear of some who are broke,
My old pardner made millions in Tampa,
While I've got my saddle in soak!

Sleeping and working together,
Eatin' old 'Cussie's good chuck,'
Riding in all kinds of weather,
Playing in all kinds of luck;

Bragging about our top-hosses,
Each puncher ready to bet
His horse could outrun the boss's,
Or any old horse you could get!

Scott lies in Tularosa,
Elmer Price lies near Santa Fe,
While Randolph sits here by the fireside
With a 'flat-face' on his knee.

'Gene Rhodes is among the high-brows,
A 'writin' up the West,
But I know a lot of doin's
That he never has confessed!

He used to ride 'em keerless
In the good old days
When we both worked together
In the San Andrés!

Building big loops we called 'blockers,'
Spinning the rope in the air,
Never a cent in our pockets,
But what did a cow-puncher care?

I'm tired of riding this trail, boys,
Dead tired of riding alone—
B'lieve I'll head old Button for Texas,
Towards my old Palo Pinto home!

N. HOWARD ("JACK") THORP

THE PHANTOM ROUND-UP

Where the city sleeps in silence,
On a soft star-silvered night
There's a soundless phantom round-up once a year,
And the city seems to vanish
In a flood of ghostly light
While the streets and shops and buildings disappear.

Then a horde of phantom riders
Spur across the starlit waste,
Where the pallid yucca flowers once again;
And the dim coulees are furtive
With the coyotes' slinking haste
While the branding fires are lit along the plain.

And the herds of ghostly cattle
Range beneath the quiet stars,
While the wary phantom riders circle wide;
Till they gather there in silence
To let down the misty bars
And corral the milling cattle safe inside.

And the shades of vanished bronchos
Plunge in rearing, snorting fright,
Shying wild-eyed on the brink of breaking day,
Till their reckless riders spur them
Into blind and panic flight,
When the eastern sky is slowly turning gray.

So the rattlers and the sage brush
And the riders disappear
When the sun climbs slowly up the eastern sky,
And the city's noisy clamor
Strikes anew upon the ear—
For once more the phantom round-up has gone by.

VIOLET McDOUGAL

CATTLE

Other states were carved or born,
Texas grew from hide and horn.

Other states are long or wide,
Texas is a shaggy hide,

Dripping blood and crumpled hair;
Some fat giant flung it there,

Laid the head where valleys drain,
Stretched its rump along the plain.

Other soil is full of stones,
Texans plow up cattle-bones.

Herds are buried on the trail,
Underneath the powdered shale;

Herds that stiffened like the snow,
Where the icy northers go.

Other states have built their halls,
Humming tunes along the walls.

Texans watched the mortar stirred,
While they kept the lowing herd.

Stamped on Texan wall and roof
Gleams the sharp and crescent hoof.

High above the hum and stir
Jingle bridle-rein and spur.

Other states were made or born,
Texas grew from hide and horn.

BERTA HART NANCE

TEXAN

To be a Texan is to ride
With past and future at your side;

To race the norther sweeping south,
And toss the dice with floods and drouth.

To be a Texan is to know
You must keep faith with friend and foe;

That men are brave and women true
Though some may fail among the crew;

That love is not a petty game,
And God is more than just a name;

To be a Texan is to feel
The Alamo against your heel.

BERTA HART NANCE

COWBOY, COWBOY!

"Cowboy, cowboy, comin' up the Trail,
Did you meet with Jerry's outfit,
Have you any word of him?"

"Yes, he drove from X-bar-T,
And he shared the tarp with me,
But Jerry'll not be comin' into town to-day!"

"Cowboy, cowboy, here's the end of the Trail,
And Jerry knows I'm waiting,
And why doesn't he come in?"

"It was when we swam the Red,
And as point-man Jerry led,
The river full of quicksand, the banks of slippy clay;

"And the current bore him down—
Oh, it's hard to see men drown—
And we cursed the old Red River and its treachery
                that day.

"Oh, it's poor I tell the tale,
How he went the long, long trail,
But Jerry'll not be comin' to dance with you to-day!"

ZOE A. TILGHMAN

THE PASSING HERD

The wind was in the south that day
A cool wind with the breath of green grass in it,
And the sunrise was full of the singing
Of the meadow lark and the wild green linnet.
Out of the creek bottom far away
Came the sound of ax strokes, rhythmic, ringing.

On the blue edge of the prairie land
Was a yellow dust cloud, like a man's hand,
Growing slowly and rising higher,
And the sunrise tipped it with rosy fire.
Softly and sweetly the south wind blew,
Slowly and slowly the dust cloud grew
Till the dim shapes of the steers showed through,
And the long herd swung down the trail
With riders at flank and point and swing,
Tall, lean men with wide brimmed hats
On quick-limbed ponies that stepped like cats;
Big-mustached men out of some old tale.
You could hear their deep-voiced "Hike-Ho's" ring
As they hazed the leaders across the flats.
And the long horned steers with rolling eyes
Came swinging along with the steady clack
Of hooves. And their heads swung back
To ease the torture of swarming flies.
And the muffled roar of the cattle bawling
Drowned out the noise of the riders' calling.

KENNETH C. KAUFMAN

LLANO ESTACADO

There shall never be brush nor pen that can tell
The haunting loveliness of the prairies nor the lure
Of the high and lonely plains that dream
Forever under the moon-glow or the low stars' gleam
Or the dim blue haze of noonday, flung like a spell
By the old gods that are forgotten, but still endure
And bide their time. There is a magic half made up of pure
And infinite distance and half of yearning pain,
Which, if a man see with his soul's eye,
From the world's edge his feet shall turn again,
Or it will drag backward at his heart until he die.

KENNETH C. KAUFMAN

THE PRAIRIE SCHOONER

When I see a prairie schooner
    With the tongue a-pointing west
What a mighty nameless longing
    Always swells and fills my breast.
For it's headed toward a country
    I shall always love the best
Toward a land of stars and sunshine
    Toward the prairies of the West.

It's a wide and wondrous region
    Naught its virgin beauty mars
Where the plains are strewn with blossoms
    As the sky is strewn with stars.
Where the air so keen and bracing
    Gives to life a joy and zest
Makes the pulses leap and tingle
    In the blood there runs the West.

And I know within the schooner
    'Neath its cover worn and brown
There are hearts with hope a-tingle
    There is faith that will not down.
Though a man may meet misfortune
    Failure never is confessed
When he mounts a prairie schooner
    With the tongue a-pointing west.

So when from the ties that bind me
    I at last shall break away,
Leave each sordid task behind me,
    As I surely shall someday,
When I choose a craft for cruising
    Love or Fortune as my quest,
It will be a prairie schooner
    With the tongue a-pointing west.

EDWARD EVERETT DALE

PRAIRIE BRAND

I'll bear forever this prairie brand
Like a canyon that cuts through a rolling land—
Deep and jagged, wild and free,
But burned into this heart of me.

I've seen where the sea bites into the earth,
Where the mountains cinch its middle girth,
Where the north wind starts on its frozen way
Leaping with gusto out of a bay.
I've felt hot winds with the singeing smell
Of cannon roaring over Hell.
I've dodged the onslaught out of the maw
When the cyclone opened its awful jaw.

I've swept over acres of bludgeoned ground
Where the deep lifeless sand can utter no sound—
No cry of complaint at the ravaging plow
That dug at the heart of the land until now,
No rusty grass bends in a westerly gale,
No quail nests, no road runner,
Naught but Death's wail.

I've seen the blue twilight, silvered, aquiver.
I've heard the land speak . . . wind, sky, and river.
I've seen the night yawning just outside my door
And heard stars sing hymns from a prairie-writ score.
Yes, I'll bear forever this prairie brand
Like a canyon that cuts through a rolling land
Deep and jagged, wild and free,
But burned into this heart of me.

VERA HOLDING

SONG OF THE FORERUNNERS

The men who made Texas
Rode west with dazzled eyes
On the hot trail of the Future,
To take her by surprise:

They were dreamers on horseback,
Dreamers with strong hands,
Trailing the golden Lion
Who couches in far lands:

Old men and young men, little men and tall,
Bad men and good men—but strong men, all.

The women who bore Texas
Could see beyond the sun:
They sat on cabin doorsteps
When the long day was done,

And they crooned to lusty babies,
But their look was far away—
For they gazed straight through the sunset
To the unborn day.

Stern women, laughing women, women stout or small,
Bronzed women, broken women—brave women, all.

The men who made Texas
Laughed at fate and doom—
Dreamers on horseback—
Men who needed room;

And the women in young Texas,
Hanging homespun clothes to dry,
Loved a prairie for a dooryard,
For meeting-house, the sky—

Wide visions and wide spaces, man and land were large
            of lung:
Texas knew not cheap and easy, slack and small, when
            she was young!

But the men who made Texas
Left their work half-done—
For nothing stands full-finished
Beneath the spinning sun;

And the women who dreamed Texas
Had much work to do
When they lay down for their last sleep
In a land still new;

And a yet-unbuilded Texas, cloud-paved and glimmering,
Burns yet before the eyes of us, who toil and dream and
            sing.

                              KARLE WILSON BAKER

THE ROAD OF MIDNIGHT PAGEANTS

This is no common roadway. Spain and France
Sowed every sentient clod with brave romance;
The cloven hoofprints of the buffalo
Outlined its course, three centuries ago,
A day when lures of water edged the wind;
The Lipans stalked them, swift and moccasined;
Conquistadores and their followers pressed
Sternly toward empire in a fabled west;
Haply, along it, as an azure flame,
Maria de Agreda's spirit came;
The gaunt Franciscan, next, with holy urge,
Bare-footed, at his waist the knotted scourge;

Then prairie-schooners of the pioneer
Led Anglo-Saxons to their last frontier.
Here surged the longhorn herds in bellowing hosts,
Spurred on, with shouting, to the trading-posts;
And gay vaqueros, singing, galloped down,
Dreaming of dusk-eyed beauty in the town.

Missions and forts have crumbled. This remains,
A memoried roadway through the Texas plains;
To either side the prairie, like a sea,
That scorns a shore, rolls vast and billowy;
And ever, when the day fails, overhead,
Stretches another prairie, starred and dread,
Where often, at the hushed and mystic hour,
The great moon blows, a silver cactus-flower,
And in its light dead centuries walk free
On this old road in ghostly pageantry.

HILTON ROSS GREER

THE TEXAS RANGER

In the old, old days when the West was young,
The Ranger rode the trail.
The thunder of hoof-beats was his song,
And the Right his Holy Grail.

He was tall and straight as Indian corn;
Weathered and brown as a berry.
His draw was as quick as the redstart's flight;
He was Law on the Texas prairie.

The sky was his roof; the earth his bed;
His saddle a ready pillow.
His friends were the quail, the wild curlew
And the shade of the button willow.

You say the Ranger rides no more?
Listen, some night, if you will
When the wind is soft as a bluebird's call,
And the prairies are dark and still,

And you may hear the pound of hoofs,
You may catch the fleeting shadow
Of a horse and rider charging across
The grassy moonlit meadow.

Through windy darkness and brittle dawn,
He follows his mighty quest,
For the trail he cut so long ago
Runs straight through the heart of the West.

MARGIE B. BOSWELL

THE SHERIFF'S WIDOW

I can see her by the window
When the evening sun is low—
Just a shadow in the twilight
Rocking slowly to and fro.

She's the widow of the sheriff,
And her hair is silver gray—
And I reckon I was one of those
Who made it turn that way.

They were living in the jail house
At the time I boarded there—
And she never failed to feed me
Or to mention me in prayer.

The sheriff was an honest man,
And "right" was all he knew—
And when he started on a job
He always saw it through.

He was firm, but he was humble.
Course he never saved a dime,
　　'Cause the county didn't pay him
Half enough for half his time.

　　Still he served them long and faithful,
Fair alike to friend and foe—
　　Stood his ground for law enforcement—
Yet the people let him go.

　　Now his widow sits and ponders
On the days when they were young—
　　How their hearts with pride were swollen
When his star she on him hung.

　　And she's happy in the knowledge
That he served with his last breath
　　The State he loved so truly—
While she slowly starves to death.

CARLOS ASHLEY

From SKETCHES OF THE TEXAS PRAIRIE

In Winter

All winter long the prairie lies remembering;
Old, old and gray, and blurred with drifting mist,
Silent and listening, hearkening to the rain,
Hearing the wind scream in its desert places.
The cotton rows stretch long and brown and lifeless,
The stubble fields are still and sad as death;
The prairie lies defeated, broken-hearted,
Conquered by winter, brooding in the cold—
Pining for fields where the tall, green grass is waving,
Longing for flowers that the springtime brings,
Brooding on other springs that are long since gone,
Brooding, and thinking of its endless past,
　　In the rain and the mist.

In Early Spring

Silent upon the prairie falls the warm rain,
Slow-dropping, dropping from the low, dull clouds.
An old, old pain long frozen in the gloom,
Tears at the bare earth's heart.
The prairie's bosom stirs; the wild, green, tender blades
         of grass come forth,
Piercing the wet, black earth where the raindrops fall
Slowly and softly like big, splashing tears.
Out of the travail and the age-old pain, the spring is born,
In tears and sacred joy, the prairie gives it birth.

GEORGE D. BOND

PRAIRIE PICTOGRAPHS

Prairie Dog

Here's a right-thinker, prosperous and proud,
Provincial, curious, insolently sure;
A town-dweller, and pleased with his home town;
Saucy when safe, but when a keener wit
Than his approaches, he will jerk his tail
(Defiant shred of dignity) and plunge
To his ancestral labyrinthine dark.

Rabbit

Droll and erratic, a jackass rabbit jumps
From form to field, or wallows in the sand
Grotesquely serious, pop-eyed, waggle-eared,
Fit for the prairie, born of it, beloved:
A Yankee critter, sinewy, strong, and tough,
To laugh at, wonder at—but not to catch.

Burrowing Owl

Ghost of the prairie, perched on the open grave
Where he was hatched, and nests, and dies at last;
Droll puff of feathers without body born;
An empty target, shedding plumes, not blood,
And curtseying when a bullet passes near.

Rattlesnake

Sinister bandit of the underworld,
Bediamonded and lithe and insolent,
Loll in the sun until the intruder hears
The dry grim humor of your rustling tail.

Spider

The tender naked spider with his rope,
The cowboy of the grass, who rides the wind;
Creator, weaving from his silent womb
A world to live in and a trap to tame
Those savage, brutal, iron-clad, venomous stings—
Air-raiders, hawks, winged, thirsting for his blood.
True poet, pioneer, soft brain among the brutes,
Who with a wisp, a dream, an intimate hope,
Meets and enslaves and feasts upon the world!

Buffalo

King of the Prairie, if all tales are true!
But your thick skull's impervious to glory,
And even an heir of empire-building blood
Must deal with flies and cows and rival horns,
Though in a zoo. A king is still a man.

STANLEY VESTAL

THE FENCE

It seemed a waste of time to build
    A fence where there was nothing yet
To keep within, with vasts blue hilled
    And flaming eyed against it set.

But when the little house was done
    They stretched bright wire that could endure
Onslaughts of silence and the sun
    And, guarded thus, felt more secure.

I know not all they would shut out
    And fancy that they could not say—
And two with desert crouched about
    Must manage things in their own way.

I think some things mirage had shown,
    Some sounds on hot-breathed wind that strayed,
Some shadows creeping past piled stone,
    Had made them need the fence they made.

But it was likely more because
    From where they came there was a fence
About each place—and like old laws
    It gave a mood of permanence.

                GLENN WARD DRESBACH

OKLAHOMA'S WILL

In memory of Will Rogers, Aug. 15, 1935

We mourn him not for repartee alone
    (Thousands there are with gift of witty tongue)
But more for something in the sharp, clean tone
    He put upon a thought, and how he swung
His philosophic lasso till its noose
    Tripped us with genial laughter, kin to youth,
And when we paused and tried to struggle loose
    We found ourselves held fast by homely truth.

But greater still, we love the simple way
    He wore the cloak of culture unadorned
With just enough of gayness to be gay
    And just enough of kindness to be mourned.
So proudly now we stand grief-bowed and still
    While all the world pays tribute to "Our Will."

                RUTH OLIVE ANGEL

SAND STORM

A snort and a shake of a sorrel mane
A whistle of fiendish rage
Then with rearing, plunging, blinding charge
The red sand whips the sage.
With blood-shot eyes and lips afoam
No bridle can hold it back,
Till the pawed and shaken prairie
Is the hue of an old tow sack.
And the new ground drilled with cotton
Is a furrowed field no more
Just a dust bowl or a wallow—
A sand-drift steeped in gore.

VERA HOLDING

TORNADO

A low-hung funnel of greyish smoke
Like a pointed freak balloon
Set out in bas relief against
A sullen, copper moon.
A hot, still brooding of lowered skies
No movement in the grass—
White, jagged lightning rips the clouds
The funnel spumes black gas!
With a whirling, deafening, maddening roar
And the speed of a meteor
It swoops, and a prairie village
Is bare as a threshing floor.

VERA HOLDING

126

IN BOURBON STREET

As I was walking in Bourbon Street
    (It was the beginning of Spring),
I heard the calling of the free airs of April,
    I heard their whispering.

And I remembered how the trees blossom,
    How in the Western brush
Redbuds make pale fires in the lowlands
    While I am a briary bush.

Redbuds blossom in Oklahoma,
    Trees bear apples and pears:
And I am bush in a stony pasture
    Shaken by April airs.

JOHN McCLURE

SONG FROM TRAFFIC

The black haw is in flower at home
The red bud's rosy tide
Splashes the wood and stains the shade
Where dog-tooth violets hide.
(Manhattan—Manhattan—I walk your streets today,
But I see the Texas prairies bloom a thousand miles away!)

Primroses burn their yellow fires
Where grass and roadway meet.
Feathered and tasseled like a queen,
Is every old mesquite.
(It's raining in the barren parks, but on the prairie-side,
The road is shining in the sun for him who cares to ride!)

The plum tree's arms are burdened white,
And where the shrubs are few
Blue bonnets fold the windy ways—
Is any blue so blue?
*(Clouds of them, crowds of them, shining through the
        grey,*
Blue bonnets blossoming a thousand miles away!)

How could I live my life so far
From where March plains are green,
But that my gallivanting heart
Knows all the road between?
(Manhattan—Manhattan—when you jostled me today,
You jostled one a-galloping a thousand miles away!)

MARGARET BELL HOUSTON

A MARCH DAY IN OKLAHOMA

Clouds today—
In ceaseless race from south to north
The fleecy masses hurry forth,
Enshrouding in a pall of dun
The face alike of earth and sun.

Wind today—
It moans and sighs around the eaves,
It rattles in the wet, brown leaves,
And now a gale and now a breeze,
It whistles through the naked trees.

Rain today—
And streaming from the sodden sky
The crystal drops come trooping by,
Which, falling thick on walk or street,
Form rivulets beneath my feet.

Storm today—
I see the vivid lightning flash,
And soon I hear the answering crash
Of thunder, which with sullen roll,
Reverberates from pole to pole.

March today—
Yet look! In yonder copse I see
A frail but brave anemone;
And so, despite the gloomy day
I catch a prophecy of May.

WILLIAM BROWN MORRISON

SPRING SONG

These small gullies are to me
Sweet with the spring's virginity.
In other meadows, other lands
The season reaches gentler hands.

There is a tamer beauty found,
In placid, furrowed, broken ground,
And there the blossoms on the trees
Seem graceful domesticities.

But here there is an untouched strength
In the round hills, and the green length
Of prairies; and the mad colored blooms
Were never born for drawing rooms.

Let me have this then, and again
See these red gullies in the rain.
These sharp, small gullies of the south
Where dogwood meets the white spring's mouth.

DOROTHY McFARLANE

FOR OKLAHOMA

I would make a song for you, Oklahoma,
Some wild, proud anthem for your loveliness.
But I! The old, sweet singers all are gone;
The giants are no more upon the earth.
And Homer's dead. There's no one left to praise
And honor you and make your name more fair.

They cry you down, my land, the little men,
Emasculated, loud, shrill-voiced with rage,
Because they know a scoop is used with cheese
Of certain kinds; have tasted vintage wines.

You are not dainty, your manners are too bold;
You are too young. Oh, far too young!
Those Greeks they talk about, those heroes past,
Were much as you, for they, too, knew their hearts,
And their desires, and satisfied themselves
As you do. Eunuch-like, it's jealousy
That makes them snicker, laugh behind their hands.

Nor have they known you, or they would recall
The redbud in the spring, the white dogwood,
And the staunch cedars, pungent-scented, green
In snows of winter and the summer's heat.
They would remember chinaberry trees,
And cottonwoods, and long, sweet afternoons
When the world's slumbrous, never turns,
And even the buzzards sleep on level wings.
They would think long of steep and purple bluffs
And broad-browed hills, the deep, slow-running creeks,
The cotton fields, the shadowed bottom lands,
Where the pecans grow—cattle on the plains,
The ruddy Herefords—and the little pools—
Oh, otherwise they would have sung of these:
Broken Bow, Kiamichi, and Cimarron,
Big Blue and Pennington and Honey Creek.

Yet they would rather sing of dirty souls,
All out of shape from city streets and shops.

Oh, proud and free and unperturbable,
Oklahoma, do you care?

DOROTHY McFARLANE

A WOMAN'S SONG

The Lord God painted the sunset
　　And hung it against the sky,
The Lord God tore up the great ribbed rocks
　　And flung them mountain high.

And I have ruffled the thin white lawn
　　To curtain the window pane,
And I have mended the broken wall
　　Uncertain against the rain.

The Lord God measured the great green sea,
　　And counted its heart in hours,
He sent his forked fire from Heaven
　　To bring him a chart of the flowers.

And I have made a rainbow thing
　　For a quilt on the worn old bed,
And I have drawn a magic ring
　　Where gentle words are said.

God made the world while lightnings played
　　Below the purple dome;
And under a low roof I have made
　　The miracle of home.

MARY CARMACK McDOUGAL

131

THE LEADER

On a summer night, when the sands were white
And the mountains blue and dim,
Old Timber-wolf called to the night
And the Night-wind answered him.
The Night-wind told old Timber-wolf—
(And Timber told the pack)—
That near the canyon's shadow-rim,
In a cabin all a-rack,
A man from the East and a man from the West
Lay sprawled on a hemlock bed;
And both were deep in a hunter's sleep
While the dim, small hours sped.

On a summer night, when the sands were white
And the Dipper to the West,
The Night-wind told old Timber-wolf—
(And Timber told the rest)—
That the door was down and the window gone
From the cabin-wall of gray;
That the fire burned low and the pulse was slow,
And the guns in their holsters lay.
They'd only to slip to the canyon's lip,
And circle a stealthy ring,
And creep and creep on the hunter's sleep;
'Twas easy as anything.

On a summer night, when the sands were white
As the face of a peering ghost,
The Night-wind called old Timber-wolf—
(And Timber called his host)—
So the wolves went down on a hidden trail,
And the wolves sneaked low and gray,
To the silver track of the canyon floor
And the shack where the hunted lay
And all would have read as it was said,

With many a shrilling cry—
A cruel feast by a hemlock bed;
But an Unseen Guest came by.

On that summer night, when the sands were white
And the prowling wind at rest,
A Something told the man from the East
And told the man from the West.
When shadow of gray pressed shadow of black—
(Now, this is what they tell)—
Two guns from the cabin went "crack, crack!"
The foremost shadow—fell.
And now on a night when the sands are bright,
The wolves by the canyon-wall,
With hungry howl and coward growl,
They call, and call, and call!

JENNIE HARRIS OLIVER

SANDSTORM

The west wind blows
The drifting sand,
I watch it sift
From a Cosmic Hand—

Dust of the stars,
Dust of the sea,
Dust of the dead,
Ceaselessly—

Mountains and men
Who left no trace,
Ride with the wind
In a dusty race;

Dark multitudes
Go swiftly by,
As I must ride,
As I must fly.

Shall I behold
The drifting sand,
When my dust blows
Across the land?

PATRICK DACUS MORELAND

PRAIRIE DAYS

*Lawton, Oklahoma, at the beginning
of this century*

Those were exciting days, stormy and turbulent,
Filled with the growing pains of a new country
Raw and gaunt as the bones of the buffaloes
Bleak by the creek beds south of the Wichitas.
Lawton, the new town, sprang from the prairie-land,
Grew as a mushroom grows . . . spawn of a cow-pat,
Sired by a dark night, wind for god-father.

Lawton, the Lottery Town. Men were there from the
    North,
From the East and West, from the South and the
    Southwest.
Some with their wives. Some with their women. Some
    alone.
Seeking new land . . . a beginning. Some looked
    forward,
Eyes filled with visions. Some looked forward,
Afraid to look back. Lawton received them.

All night long the hammers sounded . . . the hammers
of building.
Houses grew in the flare of kerosene torches.
All day long the hammers sounded. Dawn to midnight,
Midnight to morning there was no rest anywhere.
Crowds milled in the muddy streets . . . gamblers and
harlots,
Bankers and lawyers, cowboys and con-men,
Soul-savers and soul-wreckers, young men and old ones,
Building, trading, rioting, hoping, dreaming.

Out of the whirlwind came permanence . . . Smith's
Dining Hall,
The Court House, the Land Office, the Depot.
Streets were named. Flimsy houses grew along them
Like prairie weeds . . . tents and converted box-cars,
Water was hauled from springs near Medicine Bluffs
And paid for with silver. Baths were not frequent.

Out of the North came blizzards, fanged with icicles.
Out of the Southwest came cyclones, bringing destruction.
Out of the South came drought. From the East came
wagons
Filled with sunbonneted women, staring children,
chicken-coops,
Men with fixed gaze, looking Westward. The Comanche
Indians
Came from their allotments, blanketed, garish with paint.
The part in the bucks' hair was painted with vermilion.
The squaws eyed the white women's dresses with
reserved judgment.
The Apaches came from Fort Sill. Geronimo, the great
warrior,
Terror of Mexico, scourge of the Southwest, hawk of
the desert,
Sold picture post-cards of himself for dimes and nickels.
The Indians were silent and observing . . . neither hostile
nor friendly.

In the East End the honky-tonks rioted. The Painted
        Women
Leaned from their windows and ogled, leered and
        solicited.
They were not ignored. There were famous ones.
French Marie, Babe Dot, Step-and-a-Half Annie with
        a flat foot.
Kooch dancers tossed their torsos to the squealing of flutes
Played by the famous Turkish musician, Ikey Greenbaum.
Dora, the Mud Eater and Flora the Flying Lady were
        attractions
In the Tent Shows. "Ladiez and Gen'lmen . . . gather
        closer.
See Dora! Dora! She eats mud! A dime . . . the tenth
        part of a dollar."

There were eye-catchers for the curious everywhere.
Boxes covered with wire held bobcats, skunks and
        prairie hawks.
Boxes covered with glass held tarantulas, rattlesnakes and
        centipedes.
Bottles spilled rot-gut liquor more venomous than the
        vipers.
There were great barbecues . . . whole beeves turned on
        log-spits
Over the firepits. A grand fragrance of roasting burdened
        the breezes.
The coyotes smelled it, drooled and yapped their
        hungriness.
Prairie dogs barked by day, resenting the intrusion.
Buzzards wheeled, puzzled by the unusual activity.

There were shootings and swift justice. A great prairie fire
Swept from the mountains driven by a Norther.
The streets were rivers of stampeding cattle.
The sky was meteored with burning chips. The wind was
        a demon.
The Lord's mercy and the efforts of the townsmen
Saved the city, but a memory was seared forever
On the minds of the Lawtonites.

Churches lifted brave spires in the wilderness.
The women-folk gathered, talked and organized
The Euterpe Club, Merry Wives and the Entre Nous.
The Episcopal Ladies' Aid took up its good work.
There were evenings of duplicate whist, evenings of
      reading
Browning, Shakespeare and Dickens. Women drove miles
      through rainstorms
To attend the meetings. The good ladies
Curried the cockleburrs out of their husbands' whiskers
And made them presentable. Culture flourished.
The Town grew up and became respectable.

Those were exciting days, stormy and turbulent,
Filled with growing pains of a new country.
The pages of my memory book are more fragrant
For the pressed leaves of prairie grass in them.

DON BLANDING

HEALING

Once in springtime I forgot.
    (Very high and far were the white clouds flying,
    Apple trees and white thorn gorgeously ablossom,
    Violets in the woodlands and vervain on the hills.)
All the world was sweet with the surging gladness,
And my bitter memories for an hour passed away.

Once in summer I forgot.
    (Very blue and cloudless was the far-domed sky.
    Lilac time was past and the roses royal blooming,
    Vagrant breezes whispered in the full-leaved trees.)
All the world was blessed in the rich warm splendor,
And aching hardness was melted for a day.

Once in the autumn I forgot,
    (Haze of tender blueness veiled the brooding skies;
    Prairie grass was brown and sumach blazing crimson,

Dying leaves were falling in drifting rain of gold.)
All the world was glad in the harvest and fruition,
And my futile longing for a little time was stilled.

How in wintertime forget?
    (Very near and lowering bend the cold gray skies,
    Icebound the creeks where the barren trees loom
        starkly,
    And black the crows go sailing past the low red sun.)
And memories come thronging, but vain their bitterness,
For I have found love's healing, learned that joy is
        more than pain.

ZOE A. TILGHMAN

BEAUTY IS ELSEWHERE

Truly, there is no beauty in Fort Worth, no song;
Only the clamorous glad cry of the sparrows in the trees
        at the City Hall;
And the little pool at Rock Springs that tall poplars seek
        jealously to hide, with the graceful willows
        trailing their bending boughs in the silver
        water;
And the smoothly-rolling hills to the west, like those of
        Palestine.
And beside the Public Library on a January day, if you are
        fortunate, you may see the bushes sheathed in ice,
Each slender limb all wrapped in cellophane.
No, there is no beauty in Fort Worth—
Just sunsets, and rainbows, and the slanting rain;
And, I nearly forgot, the same moon that shines on
        Venice. . . .
The same stars.

BOYCE HOUSE

CITIES

Dallas,
A pompous-girthed merchant
Who, after a day of bartering among his bales,
Sits down to talk of culture.

Houston,
An old Southern gentleman,
Seated on the veranda of a mansion with white columns;
The air magnolia-scented,
Negroes singing at sundown.

San Antonio,
A Spanish grandee,
In velvet trousers and a jacket with silver buttons,
Taking his siesta in the patio of a palace,
Lulled by a light guitar and the splash of a little fountain.

Fort Worth,
A bronzed cowboy,
With spurs clanking,
A bandana knotted at his throat;
Quick to laugh, or shoot, or take a drink;
A ring-tailed tooter from Bitter Creek—
At his saddle-horn a lariat
With which he tries to lasso the stars.

                                        BOYCE HOUSE

PART IV
From Woodland and Gulf

In Arkansas and East Texas—in mountain, river valley, and along the Gulf coast—the dominant culture is the Old South in the Southwest. But here is the Old South with the pioneering spirit yet alive, the forward look of the West, with little grieving for the past. As in the Old South poetry has been primarily lyrical, so in this part of the Southwest the poets sing and have sung of tree and flower and bird, cotton fields and streams and hills, and of those who keep steady company with the land and sky.

The folk poetry of Anglo and Negro of this woodland area is poetry to be sung, often to be danced to, as the play-party songs of mountain and farm. The old British and native mountain ballads are heard in many a home in the Ozarks where Vance Randolph or John Gould Fletcher may jolt over rutted roads to record them. In Texas, too, these English and Scottish ballads are remembered. The Negro sings spirituals handed down from slave days and makes up new ballads to tell of the boll weevil pest or of the murder of Johnny by Frankie.

The poet of the early Southwest to gain most renown was Albert Pike whose "Hymns to the Gods" was published in *Blackwood's Magazine* about 1838, with "Christopher North" hailing him as "the coming poet of America." Born in Boston in 1809 (in the same year and city as Poe), he came West in 1831, first to Arkansas, then on to Santa Fe, and back to Little Rock where he made his home from 1833 until after the Civil War, in which he served as a Brigadier General with the Confederate Army. Except for his neo-classic poems to the Greek gods, he wrote of Dixie, of mocking-birds and robins, girls with pretty names, Isadore and Queridita, and gently sad lyrics such as "Every Year." An early biographer of Poe, John H. Ingram (1880), contended that the "Raven" was inspired by Pike's "Isadore."

Mirabeau B. Lamar, who came to Texas from Georgia in 1836, like Albert Pike, was a man of public importance and an amateur poet. While serving as a major general in the Army of the Republic and as first Vice President and second President of the Texas Republic, he wrote "The Daughter of Mendoza," "Carmelita," and other poems later published in *Verses Memorial*. Of the Texas poets of the Civil War period Mollie E. Moore Davis is well known for "Lee at the Wilderness" and "Minding the Gap." Seemingly the best established claimant for the famous ironic "All Quiet Along the Potomac" is Lamar Fontaine, who had been Mirabeau Lamar's secretary during Lamar's presidency. Lamar, Davis, and Fontaine are included in an early anthology of Texas poetry, Dixon's *Poets and Poetry of Texas* (1885).

Fayetteville, Little Rock, Austin, and Houston were the early poetry centers of Arkansas and Texas. Except that Houston has been supplanted by Dallas as a place for poets to live and convene, this remains true today. Following in the wake of the poetic influence of Albert Pike, in the late nineteenth and early twentieth centuries a group of professional writers in Little Rock—Fay Hempstead, Clio Harper, C. T. Davis, Fred Allsopp, and Mrs. Bernie Babcock among others—wrote and encouraged the writing of poetry, mostly lyrical, often occasional and popular. Mrs. Babcock, who edited the first Arkansas poetry anthology in 1908, is the only survivor of this group. It is of interest to note that during the nineteenth and the first quarter of the twentieth centuries in Arkansas and East Texas most of the poetry was written by men and a few women who were active participants in military, political, business, and journalistic life, and that their poems were written for the general reading public.

Writing clubs in both Little Rock and Fayetteville were organized in the eighteen-nineties and early nineteen hundreds. A number of these are still active: the Authors and Composers, the Poets' Roundtable, the Arkansas Branch of Pen Women, and the University Poets. In Dallas in 1921, the Poetry Society of Texas was organized by Therese Lindsey and others. It has grown to a membership of two thousand, with a number of affiliated groups meeting over the state. Many of the Texas poets belong also to the Texas Institute of Letters, which annually awards a prize for the best volume of Texas poems. In the late twenties Vaida and Whitney Montgomery, both poets, founded in Dallas *Kaleidograph,* a magazine of verse, and the Kaleidograph Press, devoted largely to the publication of poetry.

The outstanding contemporary poet of the Southwest Woodlands is John Gould Fletcher, who grew up in the Albert Pike Mansion in Little Rock and now lives just outside the city. It has been a long odyssey that has led Mr. Fletcher back physically and poetically to his own state—an odyssey that included Harvard, Paris, London, New Mexico, and Arizona. As one of the original group of Imagists, wherever he has journeyed and lived he has sensed color and contour and has endeavored to portray the transitory in relation to the eternal.

Glenn Ward Dresbach serves as a link between a number of the Southwest states, Texas, New Mexico, and Arkansas. He and his poet wife Beverly Githens now call home a hill-perched house in Eureka Springs, Arkansas. More than most poets who write about the Southwest, he concerns himself with people in their relationship to land and sky and weather. Many of his best poems are pastoral idylls comparable to the New Hampshire poems of Robert Frost.

The leader of the Fayetteville poets is Rosa Zagnoni Marinoni, who writes concisely, often epigrammatically, of people and places of the Ozarks. Irene Carlisle, who lives on a farm near Fayetteville and belongs to the University poets, writes poignantly of the satisfactions and heart breaks of farm life. Mary Anne Davis also belonged to this group. A volume of her sensitive lyrics, *From My Window,* was published by the Bar D Press at Siloam Springs. During the thirties this press under the guidance of Katharine Murdoch Davis, herself a skillful poet, published a number of excellent small volumes of poems. Of the younger poets of Arkansas Richard Leon Spain and Marcelle Chancellor Leath show intensity of emotion, expressed in words that freshly belong together. Many of these poets first appeared in print in John William Lempke's newspaper column "Ozark Moon," and his yearly anthology *Ozark Moon Book* (1929-1937).

Although the Texas Woodlands has produced no poet of the stature of John Gould Fletcher, a number of poets publish widely and for a quarter of a century have been known throughout the nation. Grace Noll Crowell writes technically sure, heart-warming poems of home life, nature, and religion. Karle Wilson Baker published several volumes of beautiful, quiet lyrics before she turned to fiction. Fay Yauger writes memorable poems from her farm youth. Margaret Bell Houston, granddaughter of General Sam Houston, writes both lyric and whimsically humorous verse. Lexie Dean Robertson and Patrick Moreland insert this light touch into prevailingly serious volumes. Most Texas poetry is rural, but Hilton Ross Greer and William Bard find poetry in the city, history, and legend.

The cotton lands have produced no noteworthy poet of the Negro race, but at least three Anglo poets have written of the black man with sympathy and understanding. In Arkansas in the post Civil War period Ruth McEnery Stuart, primarily known for her fiction, wrote dialect poems of the faithful Negro servant. Kate McAlpine Crady, of Texas and Mississippi, writes of the Negro with pathos and humor. The University of Oklahoma Press in 1946 published *Ziba,* a remarkable volume of Negro dialect poems by James Pipes, formerly of Louisiana, now of Norman. It is to be hoped that with improved education for Negroes in the Southwest, poetry will spring from the genius of this race.

Of the three best known poets of the Gulf, two were born with the love of the sea in their heritage, John Peter Sjolander from Sweden, and Stanley Babb from England. The lyrical, often moralizing, poems from Sjolander's *Salt of the Earth and Sea* have been often reprinted. Stanley Babb writes of the Gulf and its legends of lost ships and buried treasures. Siddie Joe Johnson grew up on the Gulf and her surest lyrics are of the waves and shore. In theme and expression, this section contributes some of the deepest emotional values to the poetry of the Southwest.

DOWN THE MISSISSIPPI

I. Embarkation

Dull masses of dense green,
The forests range their sombre platforms;
Between them silently, like a spirit,
The river finds its own mysterious path.

Loosely the river sways out, backward, forward,
Always fretting the outer side;
Shunning the invisible focus of each crescent,
Seeking to spread into shining loops over fields.

Like an enormous serpent, dilating, uncoiling,
Displaying a broad scaly back of earth-smeared gold;
Swaying out sinuously between the dull motionless forests,
As molten metal might glide down thc lip of a vase of
            dark bronze;

It goes, while the steamboat drifting out upon it,
Seems now to be floating not only outwards but upwards;
In the flight of a petal detached and gradually moving
            skywards
Above the pink explosion of the calyx of the dawn.

VI. Night Landing

After the whistle's roar has bellowed and shuddered,
Shaking the sleeping town and the somnolent river,
The deep-toned floating of the pilot's bell
Suddenly warns the engines.

They stop like heart-beats that abruptly stop,
The shore glides to us in a wide low curve.

And then—supreme revelation of the river—
The tackle is loosed—the long gangplank swings
        outwards—
And poised at the end of it, half-naked beneath the
        searchlight,
A blue-black negro with gleaming teeth waits for his
        chance to leap.

                JOHN GOULD FLETCHER

CLEARING

They cleared the field. Their shadows stride for stride
Walked early in the frosty sun of fall.
They blasted stumps, laid out a ragged wall
Of stone; and nightly he remarked with pride
How rich the soil, and nightly she replied
How broad the view, how she was pleased with all.
The year drew in; they missed the kingbird's call,
And the first furrow ripped the mountain side.
All winter, gathering in the brittle brush,
Curbing the shallow spring, tending the stock,
They stopped to look about their fallow slope
Where seed must swell and summer fields lie lush.
Their land, untried beneath its splintering rock,
Walled with their strength, deep-seeded with their hope.

                IRENE CARLISLE

PLANTER'S CHARM

Slowly Nan the widow goes
Up and down the furrowed rows,

Corn-bags chafing her waist, her hips,
As the kernels fall from her finger-tips:

"One for the buzzard—
One for the crow—
One to rot—and—
One to grow!"

Once she had dreamed (but not of late)
Of another life, of a kinder fate:

Of quiet streets in foreign towns,
Of dancing tunes, and men, and gowns.

But all her dreams were dreamed before
Tim Slade drew rein outside her door.

"One for the buzzard"—Tim was dead
With a bullet hole through his reckless head.

Tim with his cheating ways and words,
Marked from the first for the wart-necked birds,

Tim who had left her sorrowing days,
The farm, and a pair of sons to raise.

Lon was her first-born: "One for the crow!"
Where had he gone? She'd never know

For there was a price upon his head—
"A chip off the old block," people said.

Then "One to rot!" Her thoughts go back,
Like hunting-dogs on an easy track,

To the girl she'd been before she came
To love Tim Slade and bear his name,

And something as stinging and hot as sand
Slides down her cheek and strikes her hand

And she sees the field through a shimmering blur
For what has marriage meant to her

But a heel of bread in a roofless hut,
Or a crawling course through a mouldy rut?

As if in answer, over the ditch
A child comes riding a willow switch:

Her second-born, of whom no one
Could say in truth, "His father's son."

For his chin is firm, and his mouth is grave,
And the look in his eye is bright and brave.

And she, remembering farm-hand talk:
"You lose three seeds to get one stalk,"

Stands tall and proud and her pale cheeks glow
As she drops a kernel: "One to grow!"

Slowly Nan the widow moves
Up and down the furrowed grooves,

Peace in her heart and a smile on her lips
As the kernels fall from her finger-tips:

> *"One for the buzzard—*
> *One for the crow—*
> *One to rot—and—*
> *One to grow!"*

FAY M. YAUGER

SHEEP IN A HILLSIDE CHURCHYARD

Sheep in a Churchyard grazing on the graves,
Walking on padded hoofs with low bowed head,
How gently meek you move among the stones,
As if in fear you might awaken the Dead!

This is a lonely place in days like these,
When drizzling rains are falling slow and drear—
The lovely sheep are visiting the Dead . . .
(I wonder if the Shepherd sent them here?)

ROSA ZAGNONI MARINONI

CHRISTMAS IN THE OZARKS

The sky is gray,
Gray like the thin mare nosing above the grassless field.
Gray as the unpainted shack and its hingeless door,
And its cardboard-patched north window—
And its south and west windows, too.
Gray as the dusty road, the barren trees, and the
      blackberry bushes.

The corn stubble nodding in the wind is also gray
Like the cowless barn that slants northward revealing its
      ribs.
The headless scarecrow is gray,
And the snow, fast-frozen on the useless trough, is gray.

But at the east window,
The only one with a glass pane in it,
There hangs a bright Christmas wreath
Made of tiny, red paper stars caught on a twisted wire.

ROSA ZAGNONI MARINONI

THE LONG NIGHT

So early in the year it is grown late!
This dusk is strangely premature in falling;
and queerly comes a silence to pulsate
the nearness of a foe, and no jays squalling.
There is a cold presentiment in this wind
of longer, harder night than we've been knowing.
We suddenly see the hopeful harvests thinned
And hear the dry stalks of our future blowing.

Abandon quickly what cannot survive!—
the fallen leaf is but the bough's wise treason.
Only shall live what WILLS to be alive
against the rigors of this changing season.
The southbound wing instructs the heart that grieves
to rise above the death of flame-tipped leaves.

MARCELLE CHANCELLOR LEATH

AN OZARK PLOUGHMAN

Round-shouldered, lean, a man has come to plod,
And sweat all afternoon behind the plough,
On that same river-land his forbears trod,
Who lie beneath the grave-plot's cedar now.
Head bent, he walks behind the strong white mare,
Year-long the sole companion of his toil,
Watching the moist black wounds beneath the share,
Furrow on furrow in the heavy soil.
Here the whole earth is measured by a field,
Bare woods, lone graves, a cabin on the hill;
All life is measured by the harvest's yield,
By birth and death—and life is very still.
The horses of our chaos, plunging by,
Swerve from his hill-girt world of field and sky.

MARGARET R. RICHTER

HILL FARMER'S EPITAPH

I asked the plowshare resting in the strands
Of vetch, and creeper-vine, and golden-glow—
"What were the dreams he told you with his hands,
Guiding your handles down the rocky row?"
"His dream was sun and stars, and Hope's high morn;
He dreamt the golden sheaf—not his poor wheat,
And not his acre of drought-shriveled corn—

He walked uphill beyond each day's defeat."
He walked uphill at last and never turned
Backward to latch the clumsy barnyard gate,
To cross the kitchen stoop sun-bleached and burned
Or lift the tools that stand and rust and wait.
He saw gold wheat fields in a wider land,
And a bright scythe stood ready to his hand.

RICHARD LEON SPAIN

GIVE ME THE APPLES

Give me the apples from the tree,
Wine-bright and ready for their doom.
Pluck me the fruit before it falls;
Next year the frost may bite the bloom.

Give me the apples; spare the tree.
I shall not need the stark-dry bough.
Store me the fruit that I may have
Words of a promise—ripened now.

BYRON CHEW

COUNTRY AUCTION

He stands bewildered in the windy cold,
Alien now upon his forfeited land.
He sees his good axe in a stranger's hand
Hefted; his world is bidden up and sold.
The churn, the coffee mill, the butter mold,
His wagon, and the cherries Phoebe canned;
His mules, led in from pasture paths to stand
Docile beneath an unfamiliar hold.

He had not dreamed his provident years could be
Carted away in bits, nor thought to see
His stable stripped, his tended cabin bare.
Thinking how proud he led his great teams forth
He turns his eyes upon the darkening north
And snaps the harness buckles on thin air.

IRENE CARLISLE

THE LITTLE TOWN

"O little town in the rain
With the empty street
So still,
So grey and soft in the twilight,
I have a slim little brown-eyed girl
And a fat little blue-eyed boy
In that brown house there.
Do you know, little town?"

And the little town says, "I know."

"Oh little town in the rain,
Outside is the huge world
With glaciers and forests and rivers and seas."
But the little town heeds not.

Then the last foot leaves the street
And here and there
A window fills with light,
Golden amongst the grey,
And the little town in the rain,
The sleepy town,
Snuggles down for the night
Like a small plump 'possum,
Trusting its happy heart
To keep it warm till the morning.

KATHARINE A. MURDOCH DAVIS

THE TREES OF FAYETTEVILLE

Fayetteville in the Springtime!
   Sequoyah a living screen
Where trees just wakened from winter
   Are feathering into green.

Fayetteville in the summer
   Catching each vagrant breeze,
And dreaming away the hours,
   Is cool in the shadow of trees.

Fayetteville in the autumn!
   Her trees float flags of gold
And scarlet and amber and russet,
   In colors manifold.

Fayetteville in the winter,
   Supremest in artistry—
Etched against sun-rise and sun-set,
   The bare brown boughs of trees.

MARY ANNE DAVIS

THE WATER FINDER

They heard him shuffling through the maple leaves
Along the lane. He seemed to make more noise
Than necessary just to let them know
That he was coming.
                    "Cider time again!"
The farmer chuckled to his wife who stood
Beside him in the yard. "He always comes
When cider starts to wink."
                    The woman said,
"The poor thing is lonesome and he thinks
That we are good to him. Just let him talk."

"And drink our cider!"
                    "Well, last year you know
He told us how to save our apple trees
That had been blighted."
                    "But it didn't work."
"He took all day to tell us in between
His tales of Gettysburg."
                    "That's where he fell
In battle with a wound—and here he fell
To sleep from too much cider."
                    "Well, there's hay
For him to sleep on and the barn is warm."

They turned to look at him as he came up . . .
"Well! Howdy, folks! It's good to see you here
Together in the yard. The air's so fine.
I wondered as I came along the lane
What you were doing out here in the yard.
I thought I'll bet they need another well
The farm is growing so."
                    "Now that beats all,"
The woman said, "That's just the very thing
That we were thinking of. We need a well
And don't know where to start in digging for it."

154

The farmer said, "This forked stick that I hold
Gave us away."
                              "Well, well, I didn't see
That stick till now," the old man chuckled then.
"Let's have the stick. . . . Now this will never do.
You need young apple branch with juice enough
Beneath the bark to let it twist just so
When you get over water, two forks down
And one that's longer to be held like this.
Now, I'm a water finder. I've found wells
For people ever since I was a boy.
It's just a natural gift some people get.
Just let me show you, and you'll have a well."

He blustered off into the orchard then.
They saw him like a dusty sparrow staring
With head on one side under apple boughs.
"More monkey business to deserve a drink
Of cider," grinned the farmer.
                              "Let him try.
I've heard of water finders ever since
I was a girl——some people think it's true."
"Well, it won't hurt us any. If he marks
A place it may be good as any other.
This land is full of hidden springs."
                              "That place
Between the trees there would be fine to have
A well in," said the woman, wrapping hands
Up in her apron, chilled for standing long.

"That does look like a good place." He'd come back
And held an apple stick like he'd described.
The farmer said, "I think a better place
Is there between the woodshed and the gate."
His wife looked at him quickly.
                              "Well, we'll try,"
The old man answered with important air.
He tried the ground between the trees.

"See here,"

He called, "the branch is twisting in my hands.
There's water here. I'll mark the place it seems
To be the strongest."

And the farmer winked.

He said, "Now try this place that I picked out
Between the woodshed and the gate."

His wife

Gave him a side-glance that said more than words.

The old man much intent on business now
Went to the place without a word and held
The forked branch out before him as he walked . . .
"I do declare," he said, "it's twisting here.
Almost as good as there between the trees!
You'll have a well in either place. The one
That you decide on will be good enough."
He held the branched stick out to them, "Look here
How juice is twisted out along the bark.
I had to hold it tight."

The farmer said,

"Would holding it so tight squeeze out the juice?"
"No," said the old man soberly, "that comes
From force of water twisting at the branch
While it is held—just like 'lectricity
Pulling at something. It is hard to say."
"You must be chilled," the woman said,
"Come in the house while I get dinner on."
"Yes, water finding's hard. It takes the snap
Right out of me. I have to be so tense
To do it right. Just watching every second—
It's mighty hard—but you will have your well."

The woman went before them. As she turned
Into the kitchen she had heard him say,
"A little cider now would be just right."

The farmer chuckled as he got the jug.

GLENN WARD DRESBACH

HELLO THE HOUSE!

"Hello the house! Is anybody home?"

The caller leaned against the rusty fence
That drew its barbs close round Grant's eighth of land,
And quelled the dogs that raised a vicious racket—
They'd started when he first turned down the lane
And parked his Chevy near the battered gate.
He stared a moment at Grant's rambling house:
Unpainted, dark, it had been settling down
Upon itself beneath the double weight
Of years and weather, as gently as its ancient
Chinaberry had been looming upward—
A wealth of shade in summer, but now bare,
Its yellow berries scattered on the sand.
The frost had slain the flowers and bitter-weeds
And left their tangled vines and splintered spears
To give the yard a wild, forsaken look.

"Hello, hello, is anybody here?"

His friendly call got only noisier answers
From the dogs re-wakened to a sharper note.
The house itself stirred meekly; otherwise,
Stood silent—as silent as the lonely wisp
Of kitchen smoke that stained the autumn air.
Do only hounds live here, he thought. Is Grant
So deaf that he can't hear his own dogs bark?
Or angry?—One doesn't send his dogs at friends.
Well, let the mute house keep its secrets then,
He'd not be one to cry a second time!

He left the house wrapped in its own affairs,
Though as he drove his Chevy up the road
That led him home, its haunting lonesomeness
Stayed with him for a troubled mile or two.

EVERETT A. GILLIS

RED EARTH

I knew the black earth of the North
As a child knows its mother:
The black land that my father owned,
And I knew no other,
Until one dazzling sunset hour—
The South, with its red earth glowing,
And here was I in a strange, bright land
Little knowing
That I would take deep root within
This red soil, and would love it,
More than I loved the black earth
With the North wind above it.

My first sight of the red earth
Shall never be forgotten:
Sunset, and a red land
White with cotton;
Sunset, and the red hills,
And wild asters blurring
Every gully purple where
A late wind was stirring.

Always from the North a call,
Through the sweet blue distance—
Always from my father's land
A definite insistence.
But my roots have struck so deep—
Deep beyond believing
In this red soil of the South,
I shall not be leaving.

GRACE NOLL CROWELL

COTTON

I climb, at dusk, the narrow trail
 That leads me, stone by stone,
Up to the slim hill's yellow crest,
 Where broom weeds long have blown;
And there I pause and turn to look—
 A sort of good-night view—
Upon the still September field,
 Where soon shall fall the dew.

And as I look, I half forget
 Such painful things as these:
Torn fingers, aching, painful back,
 And bruised and crimson knees.
For beauty robes the restful earth;
 The toilsome field below
Is magical and calm and cool
 With green—and drifted snow!

WALTER R. ADAMS

POOR-WHITE SKETCH

His house, gaunt relic of his sires,
Slackens its hold upon the hill;
His clay-and-stubble chimney leans
To sagging roof and moldering sill.

His harsh and slanting acres wear
The tatters of depletion now,
As waste and wilderness reclaim
The fields that knew his father's plow.

His lank hog roots an avid snout
In shucks and cobs beneath the bin,
Unwholesome remnants of the crop
Of rusty nubbins gathered in.

His cows turn rough and slatted sides
To meet the chilly hilltop wind;
They give, for desultory care,
A product blue and hunger-thinned.

At night his window scarcely makes
A flickering square against the gloom;
A flame no more than candlelight
Trembles and blows within his room.

No thought of moment vexes him;
He sees no vision heaven-sent;
Idle and vacuous-faced he sits,
Rapt in the folly of content.

GRACE ROSS

BLUEBONNETS

Bluebonnets; who called them that, I wonder?
"Buffalo Clover"—born in the thunder
Of heavy hoofs—is a better name.
Gone is the Buffalo (ours the shame)
And pushed is the Clover from pasture-fields
To barrener places where still it yields
A passion of blossom, a splendor of spread
Whose beauty no traveler has credited.

Pick the fine blues, of the finest—your choice—
And bound the plains by the sound of your voice,
But as far as you look still this blue you will see,
Two oceans of turquoise in ecstacy!
Where the sky takes off the two blues dim—
One up, one down; two seas, one rim!

THERESE LINDSEY

GOOD COMPANY

Today I have grown taller from walking with the trees.
The seven sister-poplars who go softly in a line;
And I think my heart is whiter for its parley with a star
That trembled out at nightfall and hung above the pine.

The call-note of a redbird from the cedars in the dusk
Woke his happy mate within me to an answer free
        and fine;
And a sudden angel beckoned from a column of blue
        smoke—
Lord, who am I that they should stoop—these holy folk
        of thine?

                    KARLE WILSON BAKER

I HAVE HEARD WHIPPOORWILLS

You say that I have grown so strange
Since I am home to stay?
I have known shyer hearts to change
When they were far away.

The night was sweet in Kelser Park:
A yellow moon lay spilled,
And whippoorwills sang after dark
In air that honey filled.
I felt the beauty all around
Nor knew how it could be,
I laid my face against the ground
With no one there to see
Except an understanding heart
Who shared the night with me.
Life offered me a brimming cup
But I dared only taste.
That brew was far too strangely sweet,
I gave it back in haste.
It bruised my soul to give it back

And say I would not drink.
I know how breaking on the rack
Can make a drooling maniac
For I felt ancient tortures sink
Through me with every clanking link
That chained me back to sober day
Where sedate worlds move on their way.
I did not want to think or feel,
I longed to dance some giddy reel
With all the little shaking leaves
That shimmered in the scented air,
To catch the spilled moon in my hair,
To wear the lace the spider weaves.

I longed to sit upon a star
And laugh aloud to see
How foolish righteous people are
In awe of mystery.
To be a fragment of the note
That tumbled from the dark bird's throat
And strike at every lover's ear
The shivery green pain of fear,
For love is brief and time is long
To listen to a sad bird's song.
I longed to lie in the lush grass
And lure the wanton winds to pass
Along the cool white length of me
As if I were a crystal tree;
To slide down from the shining moon
On some smooth plane of sky
And lose me in a rose-drunk swoon
Where purple beetles fly;
To know for mine each old delight
That June holds hidden in her night.
(I was a little mad, I think,
When I refused that subtle drink.)

And all the while a whippoorwill
Called from a dusky tree,
Whose every aching silvered note

Was echoed deep in me.
But I have come back home again
To keep my little house,
And live the mincing nibbled years
As grey as any mouse.
Yet though my ways seem just the same,
My heart has known the heat of flame,
And I am like a wind-tossed spark
Since I have heard the whippoorwills
That sing in Kelser Park.

LEXIE DEAN ROBERTSON

BEAUTY-LAND

Kiver up yo' eye, my baby, wid yo' mammy's sleeve,
　　When de windy elemints is callin' out aloud,
Dat's de way de stars dey go to sleep, I do believe:
　　Mammy Night she kivers up her babies wid a cloud.

　　White mamma, lady mamma, she's so mighty gay,
　　　Beauty's boun' to dance at de ball;
　　But black mammy, nigger mammy, ain't a-gwine
　　　away,
　　　Nuver leave 'er sleepin' baby 't all.

All about in Slumber-lan' dey's beauty layin' roun'—
　　Layin' loose, a-waitin' for de chillen to come in;
Yisterday my baby went, an' what you think she foun'
　　But dem creases in 'er wris'es an' dat dimple
　　　in 'er chin?

　　White mamma, lady mamma, she's so mighty gay,
　　　Satins boun' to rustle at de ball;
　　But black mammy, nigger mammy, nuver gwine
　　　away—
　　　Ain't expected nowhar else at all.

Lady mamma walked in Beauty's garden as a babe;
    Same ol' nigger mammy settin' watchin' at de gate,
Trusted wid de treasure dough dey say she was a slabe—
    Oh, chillen, quit yo' foolin', 'caze de times is gittin'
        late.

      White mamma, lady mamma, she's so mighty gay,
        Boun' to greet de gov'ner at de ball;
      But black mammy, nigger mammy, ain't a-gwine
        away—
      No, sir, Mister Angel, don't you call.

Baby's gone to Beauty-lan'—de pinky gates is shet—
    So mammy gwine a-noddin', too, to gardens in de
      sky,
To view de heavenly mansions whar de golden streets is
    set,
    An mammy an' her babies will be gethered, by an' by.

      White mamma, lady mamma, she's so mighty gay,
        Boun' to grace de 'casion at de ball;
      But black mammy, nigger mammy, ain't a-gwine
        away—
      Nuver leave 'er sleepin' baby 't all.

RUTH McENERY STUART

COTTON PICKIN'

      Snatch dat cotton,
      Snatch it fast.
      Dis good weather
      Ain't gwine last!

      Tote it to de cotton house,
      Dump it on de floor,
      Suckle yo' baby,
      Den back for more.

Load it in de waggin,
Run, open de gate,
Gwine to de gin-line
To set an' wait.

Ole gin a puffin',
At twelve she'll blow,
Our time comin',
Jes rarin' to go.

Snatch dat cotton,
Snatch it fast.
Dis here weather
Too good to last!

KATE McALPIN CRADY
from *Free Steppin'*
By permission of copyright owners
Mathis, Van Nort and Company,
Dallas, Texas

CANDY PAGE

Flat on my belly,
Beside of my dog,
Turnin' de pages
Of de catalog.

Slow down at de 'cordions,
Past dat git-tar and fiddle,
On to de candy page
Nigh to de middle—

Buckets of candy,
Candy in bars,
Candy in boxes,
Candy in jars.

Pourin' over de sides,
Colored up so bright,
My mouf droolin',
Jes wantin' a bite.

I licks de pictures,
Wishin' to Gawd 'twuz so,
An' my belly so full
I can't hold no mo'.

I hongry for candy,
But they's two things I need—
Money to buy it,
An' knowin' to read.

KATE McALPIN CRADY
from *Free Steppin'*
By permission of copyright owners
Mathis, Van Nort and Company,
Dallas, Texas

DE BOLL WEEVIL

Oh, have you heard de latest,
De latest all yore own?
All about de Boll Weevil
Whut caused me to lose mah home?
    To lose mah home,—to lose mah home!

First time ah saw de Boll Weevil
He was settin' on de squah.
Next time ah saw dat Weevil
He was settin' everywhah,
    Jes' a-lookin' foh a home,—lookin' foh a home!

Fahmah say to de Weevil,
"Whut makes yore head so red?"
Weevil say to de fahmah,
"It's a wondah ah ain't dead,
    Lookin' foh a home, lookin' foh a home!"

Nigger say to de Weevil,
"Ah'll throw you in de hot sand."
Weevil say to de nigger,
"Ah'll stand hit lak a man.
    Ah'll have a home, ah'll have a home!"

Says de Captain to de Mistis,
"Whut do you thing ob dat?
Dis Boll Weevil done make a nes'
Inside mah Sunday hat;
    He'll have a home,—he'll have a home!"

Ef you wanta kill de Boll Weevil
You betta staht in time.
Use a little sugar
An' lots of turpentine,
    An' he'll be dead,—an' he'll be dead!

ANONYMOUS

FREEDOM IS A WORD

Freedom
    ain't that a word?
    Oh, it's the kind of word
    that's high in front
    an' low behind.
    Freedom is a word
    that's jus' been cross-fired.

    Lord
    that was Doomsday
    w'en they hoisted up that flag
    an' said
    that's Freedom!

Father
went to Vicksburg back in 'sixty-five
an'
got in big battle at the hill
that was so hard to take.

Oh, Father
came back in 'sixty-five
said they told him
he was a Freedom man.

But, Lord
that was Doomsday
w'en they hoisted up that flag
an' said
that's Freedom!

Father said to me:
Sonny, Freedom is like a hill
it's sometimes hard to take.
I'll tell you 'bout Freedom, Sonny
an' some hills you'll have to take.

Oh, Freedom is a word
a bent-up word
but
it's bended good
'cause it's bended
jus' lak prayer
on its knees
but, Lord, it kin straighten up!

. . . .

Times
I've seen Freedom
so mistreated
you couldn't even call it a word.

Times
I've heard Freedom
spoken so low
it was only a whisper.

Times
I've spoken of Freedom
I always had
a finger-hold on God.

. . . .

But, Lord
I'd call it a scrip-tor-i-al word
jus' 'caus it is so full o' hope
down on its knees
an' waitin' to git up.

Freedom, you know
that's a patient word
a prayerful word
an' w'en you think
it's been humbled, Sonny
jus' remember
w'en Freedom is down on its knees
it ain't been humbled
it's only buildin' ladder to heaven.

Lord
w'en they built that Liberty Bell
a man had to bend
'fore it would ring
an' same way with Freedom, Sonny
a man's got to bend
jus' so he kin learn to stoop.

I'll tell you 'bout Freedom
Freedom is a word
might sometimes be
a downstairs word
but
it sho is got
an upstairs level.

      .   .   .

Freedom is a patient word
a prayerful word
a good tastin' word
a sparklin' word
as full of Fo'th of July
as sky-rockets an' roman-candles.

      .   .   .

I've seen Freedom so raggety
it didn't have pockets
but
it was still plumb full o' glory.

Ha, Freedom kin start out
any ol' mornin'
with a li'l wad of cloud
an' one yard o' silk
an' 'fore nightfall
the world be shakin' thunder
and hoistin' up flags
fum Mobile to Jericho.

Ef'n you think Freedom
then you kin talk Freedom
an' ef'n you kin talk Freedom
then you kin pray Freedom
an' w'en you pray Freedom
I'll tell you, Sonny
you're sho lightin' a lantern
in heaven.

Lord, Freedom is a word
times an' sometimes
times I laugh
sometimes I cry.

Times I've heard Freedom
w'en I couldn't see
times I've felt Freedom
w'en I couldn't hear
but I've always knowed
Freedom was a power liftin' word.
Why, Freedom kin lift a live grown man
fum a dead level
to a plumb per-pen-dic-u-lum.

Ha, Sonny, you kin nail Freedom
on the cross
but that's a salvation word
always gittin' resurrected.

Oh Lord, Sonny
Freedom is a holiness word
always solemn an' prayerful
down in deep, dark dungeon
always glad an' grateful
climbin' among the sparklin' stars.

Freedom, that's a fire breathin' word
a bugle an' drum word
a whistle blowin', bell ringin'
man hollerin', woman weepin'
child screamin' word.

. . . .

Oh, Freedom rode on that Norah's ark
an' Freedom sailed that Columbus ship
Freedom's flown a thousan' banners
an' rung a thousan' bells
but Freedom don't need no ship to sail
no banner to fly, no bell to ring
it's already a breeze wavin' word
an el-e-ment acquainted word.

. . . .

Shake hands with Freedom, Sonny
raise your arms to Freedom
clap hands for Freedom
it's livelier than a circus parade.

Bow your head to Freedom, Sonny
it's our best Bible-ated word
so full o' hope
it don't have to move mount'ns
it's mount'n itself
an' w'en that mount'n moves, Sonny
the other mount'ns jus' stand aside
an' bury their heads in the Scriptures.

Why, thank the Lord, Sonny
for makin' Freedom a bendable word
'cause w'en you think
it's beggin' for mercy
jus' remember, Sonny
w'en Freedom's down on its knees
it's bent
jus' 'cause it learned to stoop
listenin' for voice of God.

. . . .

Yes, Sonny, you kin nail Freedom
to a cross
but it's an Easter mornin' word
a sun risin' word
always plum full o' surprises.

. . . .

Oh, times do git distressful, Sonny
sometimes the hogs go to dyin'
the earth gits bilious
an' it don't look lak the sun
ever goin' to shine
but jus' keep this in yo' mind
an' bear this in yo' heart:
Freedom is a bent-up word
but
it's bended good
'cause it's bended
jus' lak prayer
on its knees
but, Lord, it kin straighten up
it kin straighten up!

JAMES PIPES

THE INCREDIBLE FLOWER

There is a spring that never returns again
Renewing the lovely cycle of the rose;
Only once does the bud bloom, the fire burn splendidly;
Then spring goes.

Spring does not rise again to the withered stalk
Rekindling white and magic flame;
Never the same bees come to the blossoming bough
Murmuring beauty's name.

There is a spring that quickens on a night
The ultimate leaf, the incredible flower,
Dulling all after seasons with the one
Charmed perfect hour.

PATRICK DACUS MORELAND

TO A BIRD ON A DOWNTOWN WIRE

And so, with feet God meant should cling
    To woodland rafters,
You poise upon that tensile thread,
    Then loose your lyric laughters.

Yet through that thread this moment runs
    A human story
More fit for art than you might find
    In all your repertory;

A theme to make a master's song
    Defy all weathers—
But not for such light throat as yours,
    Theocritus in feathers!

HILTON ROSS GREER

TO A SKYSCRAPER

Here long ago a humble cabin stood
    To shelter Man, and here a city grew
About it where the axe had cleared a wood,
    And men built houses—greater ones—and You.

The crowds pass by and yet you stand aloof,
    Majestic in your loneliness, sublime
As a sheer Alpine peak beneath whose roof
    Are chronicled the casualties of Time.

Here Life flows past, yet who in all this throng
    Of men has raised a beauty-thirsting eye
To seek the gothic soul of you, O song
    Of iron stanzas flung against the sky?

Some day this narrow plot will bear a higher
    And you, O giant that you are,
Contemptuous of Time's corroding fire—
    You shall go down like Troy—or a falling star.

W. E. BARD

THE BOAT THAT NEVER SAILED

Like the moan of a ghost that is doomed to rove
Is the voice of the wind in Hungry Cove.

The brier bites with a sharper thorn
Than the fang of hate, or the tooth of scorn.

And the twining vines are as cunningly set
As ever a poacher placed snare or net.

And the waves are hushed, and they move as slow
As fugitives making headway, tiptoe.

For Nature remembers, as well as Man,
The time, and the place, and the *Mary Ann*.

The time, man-measured, was long ago,
Some sixty or seventy years, or so.

The place, where the sea was with light agleam,
And the shore shone white as a maiden's dream.

And the *Mary Ann* (how a prayer prevailed!)
Was the name of the boat that never sailed.

For the men who built it, a blackguard twain,
Had taken a maiden's pure name in vain.

And she prayed that for taunts, and for many mocks,
The boat would not move from its building blocks.

But the builders laughed at the maiden's prayer,
And spat on her name they had painted there,

And swore in defiance of God and man
They would launch the boat named the *Mary Ann*.

But when they stood ready at stern and stem,
The boat fell down on the heads of them;

And no one came to where crushed they lay,
And no one will come until judgment day;

For their guards are briers with thorns that bite
With a pain as keen as the sting of spite.

And their only dirge is the song of the loon,
When the sea is black in the dark of the moon.

JOHN P. SJOLANDER

SAN LUIS PASS

A Legend of the Texas Coast

I.

The wind was east, the wind was wild,
    And wilder yet the sea,
As a fisherman put out from land
    And gulls screamed mournfully,
His neighbors came to plead with him:
    The boor is on the bar,
He who goes forth comes back no more
    To trust his luckless star.
Last night the sea was calm as death
    When the sun sank down to rest;
The east was gray as a fresh-dug grave,
    And pale as a corpse the west.
The clouds were skulking ghosts last night
    And the huddling stars were dim.
Do not put forth to the grounds today!
    But their words were spurs to him.

His wife came down to the marshland shore
    As the sun was rising red
With a bright-faced lassie at her side;
    Still not a word he said.
He looked across the stormy pass
    Where waves were tossing wild,
He threw his duffle in the hold
    And kissed his only child.
He kissed his wife three times—three times
    And last upon the mouth:
May God preserve the souls of three
    And winds blow from the south!

II.

His ship shot through the angry seas
    And through the waves did plough;
The wind blew sharp as icy sleet
    Across his starboard prow.

The boor swept in across the bar
    And up San Luis Pass,
And fear was in their every heart
    For the mother and her lass.
Then she went out through the driving rain,
    And *Come back! Come back!* she cried.
O lassie, lassie, your father is dead!
    But only the wind replied,
And never a word her daughter heard
    Upon her dun sea-bed,
And no one knew the place she lay
    As the tide crept round her head.

The night closed down as dread and wild
    As the wind and sea and gulls,
And drifting on the boiling waves
    Were bits of broken hulls.
But some there were who swore they saw,
    As a light far out to sea,
A phantom ship against the storm,
    Or the cross of Calvary.
And still she calls *Come back! Come back!*
    So the village women say,
For she may not give up her search
    Until the Judgment Day.

WILLIAM E. BARD

PORTRAIT OF A PIRATE

One summer afternoon old Jean Lafitte
Tramped out along this wide deserted beach,
A dark, spectacular man moving across
The sea's blue dazzle and the skyline clouds.

He wore no cutlass dangling from his hip,
No silver-mounted pistols in his belt;
But round his neck hung by a silver chain
A golden crucifix sparkled in the sun.

And as he paced along his tired eyes roved
Over the beach, across the bright blue sea,
Into the white clouds streaming along the skyline.

And for a moment as he watched these clouds,
He dreamed they were the sails of galleons
Sweeping slowly up from Panama
With ingots of gold and heavy leather bags
Of silver and of jewels from Peru . . .

And then this old man longed for those bright years
When he had shared the sudden hellish clangours,
The fierce excitements and the tensing terrors
Of long tumultuous battles—

But he was old now, and he realized
His fighting-days were ended, and his dreams
Had gone the way of last night's wind and rain . . .
He tramped along the beach and scanned the sea,
And the tall clouds coursing up across the sky,
And a great longing kindled in his heart . . .

There were no ships in sight, not a single ship:
Only the dazzling sea that hurt his eyes,
The seagulls cruising above the beach with shrill
Inscrutable cries, the tide-line on the sand,
His shadow, and the cedars in the dunes.

And then he remembered his brief hours of triumph—
Mornings when he buried bars of gold
On lonely beaches . . . windy midnights when
His little schooner put out from Tortuga
To harry some great treasure-ship . . . and squalls
Off Yucatan that tore away his sails . . .
And autumn evenings when he swaggered through
The streets of old New Orleans in the moonlight,
Astonishing the youngsters with his tales
Of his wild raffish Baratarians—
And that slim Creole woman and her kisses . . .

But these brave days had swept into the past,
And he whom men admired and envied once
Was now a scorned and tired old man wandering
Aimlessly along a windy beach:

And now his schooner was a shattered wreck
Embedded in the sands . . . his men were gone:
He had few dreams . . .
                              And so he slowly walked
Back to his cabin, his bottle and his charts
And to the wench who kept him warm at night.

STANLEY E. BABB

HIGH NOON—GALVESTON BEACH

Blue is the sea: a glittering incredible blue
Wrought from the indestructible heart of flame;
Blue are the luminous levels of the sea,
Glowing profoundly blue when the blazing whirl
That is the sun burns up across the sky
And poises on the summit of the world.

No ships invade the glitter, and no clouds
Soar up to drift across the blinding sky;
And only long waves, webbed with veins of foam
And jetting silver spray, glide up the beach
Like lazy bright-blue dragons crawling up
Out of the deepest grottoes of the sea.

It is the Sun's moment: Man is alien
And inarticulate: And man's proud ships
And Man's exultant enterprises spin
Into the dying memory of a dream:
Flame is triumphant, burning even water
And burning the imperishable sky
And burning the unconquerable sea.

STANLEY E. BABB

SEA-HUNGER

I have a heart that is always looking for water,
Under a cliff or where pale willows rest;
Even an inland river now is potent
To hold against my torn, sea-hungry breast.

For this is the dream that the child-I-was remembers—
The shell-starred sand and the long waves coming down;
The young gulls playing above me there on the beaches,
And all of the bustle and stir of a seaport town.

I have a heart that is sick for the sight of water—
Sick for the fishing boats with their fragile spars—
Sick for the nights where a kelpy fragrance hovers,
And a salty wind blows down from the salty stars.

SIDDIE JOE JOHNSON

CERELLE

There was a score of likely girls
Around the prairieside,
But I went down to Galveston
And brought me home a bride.

A score or more of handsome girls,
Of proper age and size,
But the pale girls of Galveston
Have sea-shine in their eyes.

As pale as any orange flower,
Cerelle. The gold-white sands
Were like her hair, and drifting shells,
White fairy shells, her hands.

I think she liked my silver spurs,
A-clinking in the sun.
She'd never seen a cowboy till
I rode to Galveston.

180

She'd never known the chaparral,
Nor smell of saddle leather,
Nor seen a round-up or a ranch,
Till we rode back together.

Shall I forget my mother's eyes?
"Is this the wife you need?
Is this the way to bring me rest
From forty men to feed?"

Cerelle—I think she did her best
All year. She'd lots to learn.
Dishes would slip from out her hands
And break. The bread would burn.

And she would steal away at times
And wander off to me.
And when the wind was in the south
She'd say, "I smell the sea!"

She changed. The white and gold grew dull
As when a soft flame dies,
And yet she kept until the last
The sea-shine in her eyes.

* * * * *

There are (I make a husband's boast)
No stronger arms than Ann's.
She has a quip for all the boys,
And sings among the pans.

At last my mother takes her rest.
And that's how things should be.
But when the wind is in the south
There is no rest for me.

MARGARET BELL HOUSTON

PART V

The Oil Field

The Pueblo Indians sagely conceive of six directions, "world quarters," north, south, east, west, up, and down. From the sixth of these has come a force to transform life and scene in Texas, Oklahoma, and New Mexico: oil, called by Carl Coke Rister the "Titan of the Southwest." Before the coming of the Anglo, this thick black liquid was known to Indian and Spaniard who visited the "oil springs" for curative baths, and drank oil for medicine. But the Spaniard sought the wealth of hard, yellow gold, and the Indian was content with his traditional ways. The oil boom in Pennsylvania after the Civil War incited sporadic "boring" for oil in Texas. However, the modern oil industry of the Southwest began with the dramatic gusher at Spindletop in 1901, and has come to be the source of the greatest wealth in the region, supplying the nation with more than half of its oil.

The story of oil has largely been written in prose, fact and fiction. Only a few writers have experienced in derrick and boom town that "visitation of the divine excitement" from which poetry springs. The most characteristic poems of the oil fields are imagistic— free verse lines that make sharp appeal to the senses of sight and sound and smell and often startle the reader with the sharp contrast of beauty and ugliness. Such poems are Lena Whittaker Blakeney's "Oklahoma Oil Field Pictures," Violet McDougal's "The Oil Fire," A. E. Browning's "Tulsa, Oklahoma," Lexie Dean Robertson's "Aftermath," and Sam

Giesey's "R.I.P. Indian Territory." Jennie Harris Oliver and Therese Lindsey add philosophical comment to the sensory in "Black Gold" and "The Oil Well." Will Ferrell and Glenn Ward Dresbach see men tested, by sudden wealth, to unexpected courage or consuming greed. Their poems are short stories in verse with setting, character, and conflict. Mrs. Blakeney in "Nouveau Riche" writes an ironic drama in miniature. The Southwest story in verse would not be complete without thunder in the earth and light on the horizon made by oil. Lasting are the words of poets who record both the material and the immaterial effects of these forces in the culture of a people.

OKLAHOMA OIL FIELD PICTURES

Dewdrops glitter
In the great silver caterpillar webs
Woven among the gold-leaved branches
Of the persimmon trees.
Love vines
Spread gauzy nets of gold
Over the weeds and tangled grasses
Along the dusty highway.

Across the opalescent prairie
The skyline of Earlsboro looms,—
The latticed derricks dimly etched
Against the bright blue of the Oklahoma sky
Are like the clustered spars of ships
In a Ligurian harbor that I know.

At night
Derrick lights twinkle
Over the banks of underbrush
That edge the sandy road.
The foliage of the scrub oak trees
Is brilliantly illuminated
By the flare of the gas flambeaux—
Great banners of living fire
That hang against the sky.

Along the winding water courses
And down in the dim arroyos
Scarlet clumps of bittersweet
Blazon their color on a cool gray background
Of twisted redbud trees.

The twin oil towns
Of Rascoe and Bowlegs
Wearing crowns of steel filigree
Set with a thousand jewelled lights—

Glittering pinnacles
That splash their brilliance
On the soft black western night.

LENA WHITAKER BLAKENEY

BLACK GOLD

Where shafts bite deep in a home hillside
And wounded earth in its flame has died,
The trees are tattered and seem to be
A-drip with black dew, endlessly.
The children's playhouse has lost its way
In dismal ooze and sullied clay.
The grass is shriveled in clots of grime;
And flowers, strangled in sheets of slime.
Like soot, upon coal, is the mossy stone;
Oil dabbled, the nest where a bird has flown;
And even the stream in its shaley bed
Bears glistening ink, where it once was red.

On this spot—palsied—without a bloom—
Tanks squat like gnomes in a world of gloom;
Through veins of iron is pumped away
Old forests' blood in its rich decay.
The trucks crawl out; new roads cut deep.
Where the buried trails of old dreams sleep,
A woman sees through the sting of tears
A murky flood on the pride of years;
But the man beholds, with exultant eyes,
New fortunes made and new cities rise!

For it is the law that earth shall give—
The past must die, that the present live!
So derricks stand upon ruin's wall,
And black gold flows for the good of all.

JENNIE HARRIS OLIVER

TULSA, OKLAHOMA

I.

THE REFINERIES
(*West Side of the River*)

This is Tulsa.
Oil refineries have stations here,
Where the crude oil
From Osage and Muskogee counties
Comes to be made into naphtha and oil coke and gasoline.
This is where young chemists discuss
Cracking processes, light and heavy grades of oil,
By-products, conservation, and non-leak storage tanks.
And in a downtown office-building,
Directors speak softly of bonds, and corporations, and
           mergers.
Here on the banks of the Arkansas
Are Tulsa's refineries,
Glutting the yellow waters with their refuse.
In the evening a smoke-stack swallows the sun.
Then the lights come on,
Shining in blurred and crawling patches on the oil-
           streaked river.

II.

RIVERSIDE DRIVE
(*East Side of the River*)

And on the other side of the Arkansas,
With poplars masking the frankness of the refineries,
Are the homes of Tulsa's millionaires.
Spanish patios and Irish castles are on friendly terms
With Elizabethans and severe Georgians.
And the strident gardens of an Italian villa
Scream at the hedgerows of a New England colonial.

III.

"POOR LO"

On week-ends the rich Indians come to Tulsa
From Ponca City and Okmulgee—
From their farms,
Where derricks sprouting like cornstalks

Push their steel frames to the hot, blue sky.
The women, patient and stolid
And always shapeless with child,
Wear calico, and bright blankets.
Even purple serge suits and flannel shirts
Cannot erase the dignity of the dark-skinned, massive men.
Their eyes and hair are blacker even than the oil
That brings them wealth
And huge cars, sleek and arrogant with nickel.

A. E. BROWNING

THE OIL WELL

In Palo Pinto county, once,
I saw a well "come in,"
An amber column pushed to spray
Ethereally thin.

Two vivid opal rainbows spanned
The mist, as sheer as dawn,
And they who owned it stood beneath—
Oh, magic mist, fall on!

So precious was the virgin stuff
A fragrance seemed to dwell
Within the pungent odor blown
So widely round the well.

Was this, a million years ago,
A trillion lotus-blooms?
Distilled by what old chemistry
In what abysmal rooms?

Earth must have had us in her mind
So aptly to bestir
And store away such potent brew—
Or do we rifle her?

A city—maybe mints of gold—
A country-side's advance—
Potentially all these are in
This amber circumstance!

THERESE LINDSEY

THE OIL FIRE

The lightning strikes, a sudden blinding flash
Of forkèd fire, a rending, tearing crash,
A deafening roar that shakes the very ground,
A sharp report, a sudden crackling sound!

The tank is struck! the mounting flames leap high
In wild fantastic light against the sky
The strong steel crumbles writhing in the heat
Twisting grotesquely, savage heat waves beat

In furnace blasts along the reeling air,
The oil fields lit and crimsoned with the glare
In wild unearthly beauty. Heavy, low
The black smoke hangs above the sullen glow

In rolling clouds with red flames bursting through
The whole earth has a lurid crimson hue,
The curious crowds that gather in to gaze
In half awed silence watch the great tank blaze

In devastating splendor. Far and wide
The sullen smoke hangs low on every side.—
The giant tank boils over, everywhere
A boiling flood of flame. The scorching air

Is blistering, blinding, seething torrents flow
In red cascades of flame. The savage glow
Of molten metal smoulders, twisted, scarred
The oil soaked ground is blasted, burned and charred.

All that remains to show the great fire's track
Is smouldering ruin, shriveled, seared and black.

VIOLET McDOUGAL

NOT FOR SALE

There's a church-yard down at Ranger, just an acre,
    more or less,
Where the south winds kiss the headstones in a lazy,
    soft caress,
Where the chinaberry shelters all that sleep beneath its
    shade,
'Neath the mounds grass-grown and hidden, 'neath the
    fresh ones, newly made.
Some are there who fought for Texas in the tragic
    long ago
When the swarthy Santa Ana brought his hordes from
    Mexico
And there's some who risked the desert when the great
    red West was young
And whose deeds are still unwritten, seldom told and
    seldom sung.

Flowers bloom and die at Ranger in that sacred acre lot,
Jessamine and wild rose linger lest the sleepers be forgot.
Here and there a broken bottle holds a spray of withered
    bloom,

Bits of colored glass and china brighten up some sombre
     tomb.
And, above it all, a belfry casts its long, lean shadows down
Like a hand outstretched for silence to the clamor in the
     town.
When the western dusk has fallen, springs a ring of
     garish light
And the fevered pulse of Progress beating tireless, through
     the night.

All around the quiet church yard and the meetin' house
     beyond,
Is a hedge of blackened derricks where the monster
     drills respond
To the tug of groaning cables as the beams nod to and fro,
Delving deeper—ever deeper to the treasure far below.
Tanks attest the wealth of Midas, pipe-lines strain to
     hold the flood,
There's a prince's ransom wasted in the sloughs of
     amber mud.
Yet the cry is "Give us leases. Every acre means a well.
Crowd the grave-yard over yonder. Force the board to
     lease or sell."

All of oildom knows the answer, when the chairman
     shook his head,
Gazing past the man of millions, at the city of the dead.
"There is room enough in Texas"—here he waved his
     palsied hand—
"There are countless acres open and there's oil in
     every sand.
Why disturb the weary tenants in yon narrow strip of sod?
'Tis not ours, but theirs—the title vested by the will of God.
We, the board, have talked it over, pro and con, without
     avail.
We reject your hundred thousand. Merriman is not
     for sale."

Down the long sand trails of Texas, when the great red
     West was young,

Men have fought the savage desert where now thriving
   towns have sprung.
Where the busy derricks rumble and the drills bite keen
   and deep,
Many bones today are bleaching, where these martyrs
   fell asleep.
Yet, above the trampled prairies and the oil man's
   reckless tread,
Texas still may flaunt her banner. All her heroes are
   not dead.
And that Baptist church at Ranger, old and dingy,
   half decay,
With its belfry shadows falling on its plot of precious clay,
Is a monument, eternal, on that long, dim Texas trail,
Standing guard above the grave-stones in a lot that's
   "Not for Sale."

WILL FERRELL

R. I. P. INDIAN TERRITORY

Strange, mourning genii ranked across the sky,
From prairies derrick-sown the smoke lines crawl:
And there are ebon shrouds writhing as high
Where, raw and growing, the new cities sprawl . . .
No minor litanies these fumes inscribe:
They are the last rites for the last frontier
Gone with the bison and the cheated tribe,
The buckskinned hunter, and the slaughtered deer.
Such palls have covered buffalo-grass and oak,
And lights, not flowers, in their shadows bloom:
They are grim answers to the tepee-smoke,
The shielded outlaw campfire, and the plume
Blown out above the squatter's hut that broke
Into his dream's fulfillment and his doom.

SAM GIESEY

THE NEEDLE'S EYE

Neither a woman nor a man long poor
And humble, used to taking things that come,
With wealth thrust quickly in worn hands, can pass
Into the Kingdom of the Rich—no more
Than camels can pass through the needle's eye . . .

Josiah had been told, with doubting eyes,
That he was worth a million dollars. Then
He put away his hammer and his saw
And went to see the oil well on his land
That had been worthless for so many years
Of aching toil, and with him went his wife
In bright new calico, too awed to speak.

They saw the source of this strange wealth that came
From ground that failed to give good crops, but still
They could not understand all that it meant . . .
Upon the way home through the heated dust
Josiah told his wife that she could have
What she had wanted, and they talked about
The fine hotel that they would build in town
When they had sold the plain board rooming-house
That for a year had driven want away,
When men rushed to the little town to drill
For oil . . .

                      Now in that little town it's told
How old Josiah laid his tools away
And took no care for odd jobs waiting him,
And then grew restless when a crew of men
Began to build his fine hotel—and charmed
With wages higher than his dreams had known,
He went to work upon his own hotel
For day's pay and, while working overtime
For further profit, died . . .

                 And it is told
How his old wife, with eyes that hid their tears,
When the hotel was finished took a room

That was the cheapest, and kept on at work
About the place in utter loneliness.
With only one extravagance in all
The years she lived: Josiah's picture there,
Enlarged and framed in gold, beside her bed.

GLENN WARD DRESBACH

AFTERMATH

The boom has come and thrived and passed away.
Now scattered through the dirty little town
Are left
Strange piles of huge unwieldy tools,
Grown mossy red with rust,
Misshapen skeletons of blackened derricks;
The grime, the soil, the litter,
That five thousand oil-mad people
Leave
In a town built overnight.
The silent street drags through its crooked length;
No more the echo of the mule-team's clanking chain,
No more the vibrant throbbing of some gusher newly
            made,
Only, comes now and then,
The intermittent buzzing of one last refinery.

Plodding down the scarred road
Is a man, sweat-stained and weary.
He leads a bony, drooping mule,
And at each step
The dust puffs up with little choking plops.
He had a fortune made in leases once,
But now
His prosperous farm is left a stretch of sodden greasy
            pools
With dirty yellow stubble, wilted when the crude oil
            sprayed.
There is no shade.

193

The hot sun spreads a brassy glare
On all the harsh unlovely scene.
The tin roofs crackle in the heat,
And rubbish curls in loathsome ugly heaps.
The rough unpainted shacks are hovels now,
Grey with ashy dust;
Their windows leer upon the streets with silent
Hating.
The strident voices late jarring through their walls
Have spread the rumor of another rush
And then have gone their eager seeking way.
The dance hall is a heap of blackened ruins
Where fire has held the last mad jubilee.
The pool rooms, too, are voiceless:
The whirring wheels have hushed their stirring,
And fat evil-stomached spiders spin a dusty web
Where shining mirrors hung.

These things are the last tribute that oil leaves
With her dead.

LEXIE DEAN ROBERTSON

"NOUVEAU RICHE"

"I like your Mah Jongg set so much; I saw
Another one just like it at the Waites'."
"Indeed you didn't! This is one of four
Of that fine make in the United States."

"Your dog is dead?" "Oh, yes, poor Mimi died."
"From dear old England—brought her this last trip;
I paid six hundred dollars for her, too."
"Yes, the Majestic is a lovely ship—

I met such charming people—saw so much
Of Count Le Noir, and Lord and Lady Mount;

We dined and danced together, and played bridge—
I was the favorite partner of the Count."

"My fortune? Ah, not he! Wealth gives entrée
Into exclusive circles, though, you know—
Old families on both sides of the sea,
People who've always been *comme il faut.*"

"You like my Paquin gown? I have six more;
And all my brilliants—'diamonds' here you say—
(She called them 'sparklers' not so long ago)
They came from Paris too—Rue de la Paix."

"Don't speak of Oklahoma as my home—
New York is small enough for me, my dear;
I come out west on business, not from choice—
Nine oil wells drilling! I *have* to be here."

"I hardly see how you can stand this place—
It seems so crude, it gives one such *ennui.*
You really ought to travel more, my dears,
And get away from all this bourgeoisie."

("Marie, more coffee, please——and bring my maps.")
"Here, look at all the red. It's such a bore!
We've struck the Wilcox sand at last." "Oh, yes—
That means for me at least a million more!"

"Yes, all my plans are made—I'm off again;
Paris, Vienna—maybe Italy—
The London season. . . . I'm expected there—"
"You're going?—Fold the maps, Marie.—Goodbye!"

.   .   .   .

They went out in the night—her girlhood friends—
The glorious western night no wealth can spoil;
The wind blew from the prairies, fresh and clean,
But—was it whim?—they smelled the taint of oil.

LENA WHITAKER BLAKENEY

PART VI

The Sky

From the beginning of patterned language until our own century, poetry could categorically be divided into two groups: poems of the earth, and man, the earth treader; and poems of the sea and rivers and the men who dared to put out from shore to seek other shores. Now a third classification is being born: poetry of the air. In the past, to be sure, men have scanned the heavens and, earth-bound, sea-bound, have written yearningly of the blue distances. So new is man's traversing of the sky that he employs chiefly words borrowed from land and water travel: airship and airport, pilot and navigator, air lane and air field.

The level, treeless terrain of vast areas of the Southwest offers training and landing fields for the civil and military; and months of sunshine provide good flying weather. Randolph Field in San Antonio, "the West Point of the Air," is only one of many military training fields in the region. San Antonio, Dallas, Fort Worth, Oklahoma City, Albuquerque are all important air centers. Every town has its landing field. Oil companies keep their own planes and pilots for rapid travel from oil field to oil field. Ranch men have landing strips on their ranches, locate herds, and even hunt coyotes from planes. Southwesterners have always been travellers, welcoming speedier horse of flesh or steel or flying wings.

In the Southwest, which has been defined as the region where "the sky is the other half of the world," poetry of the air is being written—not a large body as yet, but distinguished in quality and lyrical in nature. Goldie Capers Smith, whose husband was an aviator, has written often from her own viewpoint as a flier's wife, afraid yet proud; and from the viewpoint of her pilot husband as she experienced vicariously the "majesty of space." Others, too, men and women, young and old, have written of flight in the "ultimate machine," the welcoming hangar, the prairie boy's dream of being a pilot, and of the young aviator who pierces the clouds.

Radio, television, and the whirl of the airplane motor have become an accepted part of our daily living, cancelling time, diminishing space, and opening new horizons to the mind and spirit. Poetry, even here in the Southwest where we are quick to accept the new, is only beginning to voice these epoch-marking changes by which the sky becomes truly for all "the other half of the world."

PRAIRIE SKY

Sometimes for days one can forget the sky
That god-like, indifferent, never fails to bless
With unflawed beauty our huddled littleness.
One can forget—the meddling breeze goes by
Piling vacant lots with waste to catch the eye;
Or mud, or dust, or merely the heat that shows
In quivering air, can make the senses close
To everything that is far or vast or high.

Then a scrap, a bird, the casual glance beguiles
Up, up, up!—till once more, swiftly, surely,
The clean, keen blade of ecstasy stabs purely;
Oh, glorious blue across which clouds are blowing,
Or lucent gray the far rain-tempests showing,
Or sunset blazing for ten thousand miles!

MUNA LEE

CLIPPED WINGS

Bright as a scarlet tanager above
The spring-green leaves, an airplane gaily flew,
And soared beyond the glistening spires . . . I love
This flash of joy into the depths of blue.
My city's streets are very straight and gray
With houses in long rows, and close-clipped grass
Before the doors. We do not run and play
Nor shout, but slowly, soberly we pass.
    I walk dull pavements with a gentle tread,
    There are no turns in streets so close and long,
    And I am but a bead upon a thread,
    Except that sometimes I can hear a song:
    Sometimes against the deepest blue of sky,
    I hear the free and scarlet wings go by.

MARILLA MERRIMAN GUILD

THE OCOTILLO IN BLOOM

A flock of scarlet birds
    Against the deep blue sky:
With every wing outspread
    And yet they do not fly:
        They flutter there
        And poise in air.

A flock of scarlet birds
    Above a world of gray:
The only lively tone,
    In all the desert's sway.
        They flutter there
        And poise in air.

A flock of scarlet birds
    For spring is on the wing,
In tune with silent stretches
    And yet they do not sing.
        They flutter there
        And poise in air.

MARILLA MERRIMAN GUILD

RADIO

We have picked the pocket of silence. By this feat
Is set another pace for light to beat.
With coil of silk-covered wire to snare a song
Between whose breaths a thousand miles belong!
We brand our sounds and loose them pigeon-free
And practice on them some new falconry.

THERESE LINDSEY

THE AVIATOR

Climb the glittering stalk of the wind,
Pierce the clouds with their silver lining,
Prick your wings on the keenly thinned
Golden points of a planet's shining.

Shout with the stars, laugh with the sun,
Let the arms of the dusk enfold you,
But O my dear, when your flight is done,
None of these things can ever hold you.

One low roof in an earthly town,
A door ajar, and a woman waiting,
These are the things that will call you down
From the ecstasy of your heavenly mating.

Willing you come, and glad you are,
But she, who is sure of you, still is knowing
That she has a rival in every star,
And in every silvery wind set blowing.

GRACE NOLL CROWELL

PILOT-SONG

In stately rank beside my winging craft,
The clouds, a gallant troop, go marching by
In moving silhouette, an endless file
Against a painted screen of jasper sky;
And silently, below, their shadows pass—
A phantom host that does not bend the grass.

GOLDIE CAPERS SMITH

A PILOT TO A HUNTER

I cannot kill a splendid thing that flies:
I, too, have met the north wind, razor-keen;
And, isolated, where the daylight dies,
Have watched the shadows closing like a screen
Above the earth, leaving me face to face
With the unrivaled majesty of space.

Comrades, we share the miracle of flight,
Adventuring to heaven's outer bars;
Brother to comets, kindred of the stars,
We trace a path of life upon the night.
I cannot wound a throbbing, flying thing—
I know the terror of a broken wing!

GOLDIE CAPERS SMITH

AVIATOR'S WIFE

You came with a blinding flash of silver wings,
Majestic as some fabled bird of old,
Turning aside each futile flying dart
Sped of the taunting sun's own sharpened gold.

The taut-stretched earth in welcome joyfully
Leaped up to greet a spirit from afar,
Your head was haloed with unearthly light,
Your brow was patterned with a burnished star.

Then I, a quiet creature wrought of earth,
In habit, sober as my native dust,
And shy as twilight woodland creatures, came,
Beheld your splendour, loved—because I must.

My worship kindled fire within your heart,
But love and I, with cruel blades of fear,
Severed your wings and bound your errant feet,
Hoping to keep you fast, forever near.

Too soon the radiance faded from your eyes,
And lines of longing etched your patient face,
Your shoulders sagged beneath the heavy load
We brought to you of daily commonplace.

I give you back unto the jealous sky,
I yield you to the morning's rosy wings,
I watch the vistas widen in your eyes;
Your feet go bounding with a step that sings.

GOLDIE CAPERS SMITH

THE HANGAR

Home are the wings that flashed in the brazen sun;
        Still is the song that thundered against the sky;
Asleep the shining traveler that has done
        Battle with wings where man and the eagle fly!
And out of infinite night the starlight burns
        Dully on hangar walls that hover and brood,
Housing the slumbering ship as the earth turns
        Quietly in the night, in the solitude.
This is the gracious haven, the eagle's nest
        Bound to the earth in patient concrete and steel,
That watches the wild heart home, the bright unrest
        Surge from the blue, and sighs—content to feel
The safe wings tucked—and broods in the starlight's
        gleam,
Proud guardian of the immortal dream.

RICHARD LEON SPAIN

202

TO WILL ROGERS AND WILEY POST

But yesterday they walked the common way;
Today they are a part of all tomorrows,
Such souls sing not in choirs of patterned praise,
But merge with universal joys and sorrows.
For one shall fuse with all the shapes of laughter
Where simple man in peaceful leisure dwells,
And it may be that all the sweet hereafter
Shall tinkle with the kindly Jester's bells.

And one shall come in tongues of fire re-singing
The Viking song of Freya high and clear
Whenever man shall send his star-ships winging
Against the dragons of the stratosphere.
Such souls are beacon lights to all the free
Whose dreams plough furrows in immensity.

LILITH LORRAINE

NIGHT FLIGHT

Into the starlight beyond all sense of place,
Into the cone of darkness and out of time,
I soar beyond the thunder through desolate space
With wings that finger the air, then poise and climb.
Here there is only speed, there is only the feel
Of the whirling engines' rhythm, the cylinders' roar
Eating the ambient shadow, the living steel
Triumphant over the void as on we soar.
Here at last is the ultimate machine,
Metal and space fleshing the human bone,
While the blood surge, the engine blast, and the
                ailerons' keen

Skirl into a song: the pilot and plane are one—
Out of this flesh and steel a meteorite
Flaming once more across the gulf of night.

ARTHUR M. SAMPLEY

A PRAIRIE BOY'S NEED

Under a bubble
of summer sky,
the crawling tractor
and plow go by.

Ahead, the stubble
of wheat engraves
a prairie pattern
of russet waves.

Behind, unroll
the furrowed trails,
chestnut-brown
as ground squirrel tails.

But the boy at the wheel
sees none of these.
He hears above
the tractor wheeze
the beat of wings,
and his eyes are on
Marauders flying
in echelon.

Plow and tractor,
furrow and seed,
how can they answer
a prairie boy's need
to thunder through distance,
shod with speed?

RUTH AVERITTE

RAINDROP

I wonder what a raindrop is?
I fancy with a smile
The drop that splashed me may have come
Out of the River Nile.

Perhaps it is atomic might,
Extremely scientific,
Caught in a net cast by the sun
Into the great Pacific.

The problem of analysis
Is left for you to settle;
I like it better where it fell
Upon a white plum petal.

ROBERT LEE BROTHERS

FORCES

The plunging streams go bridled
To pastures of the sea.
The docile land stands harnessed
By human mastery.

But the air is charged with tempests,
And molten mountains hide
Their wrath with snowy summits,
Aloof, and dignified.

Earth's wild, primeval purpose
Ignores man's vain intents,
And tramples mighty nations
When moving continents.

ROBERT LEE BROTHERS

PART VII   *War and the Aftermath*

The picture of war in Southwestern poetry is drawn from the images of activities at home and abroad. Behind the imagery and because of it are the assertions and the questions which justify, condone, and condemn war as man's greatest achievement or his unpardonable sin. Across the five state area, poets speak their thoughts, which are not those of individuals but of groups—families, communities, the nation. When Witter Bynner writes, "Dead in the Philippines are they, These boys . . . born in Santa Fe," he is speaking the loss felt by all the families of men in the 200th Coast Artillery, those earliest martyrs of the fall of Corregidor and of the death march on Bataan. When Keith Thomas writes of the shadows war casts upon a child's mind, he is not expressing personal thoughts, but the thoughts of all who share responsibility for the kind of world children live in. Keith Thomas was killed in action in 1944, while serving with the Third Army in France. In addition to Keith Thomas, the writers in this section who served in World War II are A. L. Crouch, Everett A. Gillis, Arthur Sampley, Alan Swallow, and Charles Wiley. Tom McNeal saw service in the First World War.

Charles Wiley, who served in the United States Navy during the South Pacific campaigns, brings the reader into the front line of war at sea, with his "Don't shoot, Don't shoot! It's ours; by God, don't shoot!" A. L. Crouch reveals the lonely thoughts of a sentry on watch. David

206

Russell's poem looks beyond the strife of the present to tomorrow's dawn in freedom and peace. Like other poets in uniform, Alan Swallow hopes that he has served to worthy ends, not to uncertainty, though the matter sometimes rests in faith, as Arthur Sampley makes clear. Everett A. Gillis catches the sweeping movement forward of men in all walks of life as the "ugly task at hand" calls them to defend America. And Tom McNeal voices the resentment of older men who cannot join this forward movement.

Some of the keenest criticism and also the strongest convictions about the nature of war are expressed by women poets. No soldier could be more ironic about the causes of war than Margaret Fox Thompson in "Study in Metal," and no man could write of a son as Rosa Zagnoni Marinoni and Alice Gill Benton write. Only a wife or sweetheart could fill in the gap between parting and homecoming with the imagination and emotion expressed by Thelma Breithaupt Cash. The spiritual strength of women flows into men, who face the physical hardships: Lexie Dean Robertson, Fania Kruger, and Peggy Pond Church find the cry of life insistent before the whisperings of death. The reader of "War and the Aftermath" will discover no flight from the realities of war or careless banner waving, but strength when it is called for and faith in the better life purchased by sacrifice.

LETTER TO THE PEOPLE

You don't know me from Adam, America, but I'm part
      of you:
Farmer, doctor, fullerbrush man,
School teacher, grocer, policeman—
I'm a cross section of the land!

I'm the one you spoke to on the street with a friendly nod,
I'm the one you argued with in the public library on
      politics, as if we both knew what we were talking
      about,
I'm the one who gave you a light when you didn't have a
      match,
I'm the one who gave you a hand with a flat tire on a
      blistering August day . . .
The one who suddenly was gone from the busy routine of
      your life.
For a high bugle called me, America, a sharp full reveille,
Quick and strident,
That I could not fail to answer!

Listen awhile, America. I speak for a million others
      like me.

I am a rookie:
I was there on that chilly April day when the long line
      of raw recruits
Straggled up the muddy company street,
Nervous, motley in street clothes, awkward and scared.
Someone shouted from a barracks window:
"Here come more of them Texans:
These damned Texans will have to lick this war yet!"
The rookies laughed, yelled back,
And marched on past, their shoulders squarer, their
      hearts lighter.

I am a sergeant in a training center:
This is my philosophy:
"Give 'em hell, sergeant,
Put the fear of God and sergeants in their hearts!
Lash them with the edge of words,
Blister 'em like a mule driver,
Make 'em tough,
Make 'em soldiers."
That's the drill field, but duty hours over,
A kind word how to get along,
Or a wise crack about the higher wisdom of certain
        rookies,
And they're saying,
"The sarge ain't such a bad guy after all . . ."
Not such a bad guy—

I'm the man with a college degree
Learning to kill where once I learned the liberal arts,
And stumped the campus in high campaigns for peace;
With mind mature and seasoned,
Saw man's follies and humanity, his heart-searchings, the
        laughter of his spirit,
And felt his brotherhood.

Yet now blood steps to the cadence of the march,
Hands grow alert and adept with weapons,
Muscles and sinews quicken to the rigorous discipline of
        fighting,
Culture and tolerances are traded for the primitive
        realities of war.

I am the boy who left his girl behind:
Helpless and tangled, like a raveled banner,
Love's severed strands
Whip in the cross winds of the war!
Alas, the splendor of our passion,
Fired brightly by the torch of slow caresses,
Formed for one poised moment—
Shattered . . . frustrate . . . unfulfilled.

Weave, weave, faith of my heart,
Weave a new web of dreams,
Gather the shining filaments ripped by the brutal shears
        of war,
Thread them and weave them again,
Catch and bind each colored thread,
Fashion the ultimate pattern.

Yes, America, I'm a cross section of democracy:
I am the plodder, the gold bricker, the incorrigible,
The bungler, dreaming of medals at night, but tangling
        his feet in a column right in broad daylight,
The weakling, carrying his pretense of courage like a chip
        on his shoulder,
The simple, ripping his enemy's belly wide because the
        bayonet has the cunning of his favorite hunting
        knife at home.

Yes, America,
I am the quick, the sure, the romantic,
Taking the hardships in my stride,
Flying my thunderbolt of a plane with one hand tied
        behind me,
Fighting with flags in my heart and banners in my eyes.

Yes, America,
I am the peaceful citizen forged like a weapon for the
        battle,
Sharp, tempered, proficient, and ready
For the ugly task at hand.

America, I shall not fail you!

EVERETT A. GILLIS

FURLOUGH

Where 'ya been, soldier?
Tell me where.

In the Aleutians,
Cold up there.
Feet got frozen,
Hurts to walk.
Tired of fightin',
Rather not talk.

Goin' home soldier,
Goin' where?

Goin' to Jersey,
Folks live there.
Gonna get plastered,
Sleep a lot.
Wanta have fun
What time I got.

Goin' back, soldier,
Back up there?

Goin' back, mister,
Don't know where.
Back to fightin',
Ain't that swell?
Goin' back, mister,
Back to hell.

MARGARET FOX THOMPSON

STUDY IN METAL

The jungle shades are hiding now
A Tennessee Marine.
His pose would make you wonder how
He made the football team.

His helmet is in place, and yet
His head is bent . . . how strange!
His fingers on his gun are set.
(He'll never find his range.)

The bayonet that pierced his side
He long has ceased to feel;
But jungle shadows cannot hide
Its blade of U. S. steel.

MARGARET FOX THOMPSON

SEVENTH SON

A man too weak of sinew
    To make a seventh son
Has sinned against the Holy Ghost
    And courts oblivion.

Three for mill and workshop,
    Three for battle plunder:
One alone to call his own
    And stare upon and wonder.

TOM H. McNEAL

KILLED IN ACTION

Oh, it was very much like you
So suddenly to rend in two
The misty veil of space and time
And snuff the candle ere your prime.

For you were never that weak kind
Who waits for age to leave him blind—
Who stumbles up the magic track
Rheumatically, with bended back.

Bonne chance!—And keep an eye for me—
I'll totter in at eighty-three,
And lean eternally on you,
Who slipped away at twenty-two.

TOM H. McNEAL

FOR MY INFANT DAUGHTER

Dear child, child of the human night
The starless beaming of our fear,
Error, ingratitude, and war—
Dear child, I grieve for your birthright
Beneath these heavens: see, this year,
How blind, how deep the wound and scar.

What shall I offer besides love
And gratitude? What counsel give
Upon a planet hot with blood?
May you grow wiser than the dove
Whose passion, warm but relative,
Sits like a leaf, and the leaf's bud.

May you grow beautiful with grace
Of limb and movement; may your mind
Grow fonder of the time's decease
Than of its habitual, easy place—
More than conservative, to find
That more than earthly blessing, peace.

I hope too much? Yes, hope for all
That state, my human child, which shone
In many eyes, when the world shook,
And is not dead but yet may fall
On you, dear woman worthy grown,
On me, grown worth your backward look.

ALAN SWALLOW

AT SUNRISE

They pushed him straight against the wall;
The firing squad dropped in a row,
And why he raised upon his toes,
Those men shall never know.

He wore a smile across his face
As he stood trimly there,
The guns all aiming at his heart,
The sun upon his hair.

For he remembered in a flash
Those days now past recall,
When his proud mother took his height
Against the bedroom wall.

ROSA ZAGNONI MARINONI

ASK OF THE RAIN

We have gone forth like winds; on lost Bataan,
Deep in New Guinea's jungles, thunder-high
Above Australian reefs, we rode the dawn
Blanching across the long Pacific sky.
Search for our bones on steaming Burmese coasts
Or track our smoke plumes through Tibetan snow
Or trace the pattern of our shivering ghosts
Along Attu when Arctic winters blow.
Hearken above the North Atlantic's roars
For motors limping home to friendly lands,
And when you reach Tunisia's darkened shores
Filter the waves and sift the desert sands.
Kindred who seek us through the world's wide ends,
Ask of the rain and thunder, ask the winds.

ARTHUR M. SAMPLEY

SENTRY

I never knew a night could be so long,
    Until I walked with rifle on my shoulder
    The hours when shadows deepen and grow colder;
The hours when darkness comes down swift and strong;
The hours when silence, like a leather thong,
    Binds everything into a velvet folder,
    While nothing moves, and only Time grows older—
Until some night-bird stirs its throat with song.

I never knew a night could be so lonely
    Until I stayed awake for many men;
And through the hours of darkness challenged only
    One who had been to town and back again.
But when I thought the night had come to stay,
The stars began to burn themselves away.

A. L. CROUCH

THE WHITE BENEATH

Don't shoot, don't shoot!
It's ours; by God, don't shoot!
That underside,
That belly's ours, beautiful and large, and streaming
        aft;
High lying, high strung,
That whole lineament, and the grace she wears.
Those wings cut sharp,
The stubby nose cut blunt and rude,
Mindful of the speed she bears.

I know, I know,
I know that they have sleek ones, too.
But their low fins
And small sharp profile give
An obtrusive feeling to it all.
Theirs impregnates jealousy
Theirs seems to covet through the frame
Something which might
But never could have been.

They're hard to tell apart sometimes;
But when they say
Identified, shows IFF, shows friendly light,
        don't shoot.
DON'T SHOOT!
That white beneath, that star that's home to us.
See it now, he's flipped his wing up, tilted it so
We can see it clear
You can make it out—
God! they're near.
He's passed.
Thank God at last
He's over. Over!
Shoot!

CHARLES WILEY

DEAD IN THE PHILIPPINES

Dead in the Philippines are they . . .
These boys who, born in Santa Fe,
Spoke Spanish here, spoke Spanish there,
Have now no language anywhere—

Save as the dead speak after death,
With an acute mysterious breath
At sudden times of night and day,
Some of the things they used to say.

WITTER BYNNER

SAMURAI

How tall and slim he stood against
    The alien sunset sky,
His pale face calm, though his captors held
    The sword of the Samurai.

He raised gray eyes to the golden clouds
    And the blue hills far and dim;
Drank in earth's beauty which so soon
    Would glow no more for him.

The swish of sword! A sacrifice
    To the Juggernaut of war.
A slender pilot scales the peaks
    Of shining clouds no more.

ALICE GILL BENTON

CIRCUIT

Leave-Taking

Lost in the nothingness of time, we stood
Beside the platform and the mail
And watched the curve of sudden smoke
And heard the tingling of the rail
And spoke the empty, ugly word
In a single tear-strained breath:
"Good-bye.....good-bye, my love."

That was the pain of life, not death.

Interim

Alone in the darkness of war, I stood
Beneath tree-tangled jungle sky
And watched the streaming earth turn red
And heard the killer's thirsty cry
And saw long pieces of my flesh
Curve on the blade of a bloody knife.
"Good-bye.....good-bye, my love."

That was the pain of death, not life.

Home-Coming

Silent in the moonlight, now I come
Through land my fathers knew
And watch the hills against the sky
And see the clouds roll white and blue
And hold your name upon my lips
The treasured word of every breath
No more I speak, "good-bye, my love."

This is the strength of life, not death.

THELMA BREITHAUPT CASH

WAR AND THE FARMER BOY

"I shall come back some day," he said,
"Perhaps in time to harvest grain,
Before the sumac leaves turn red
And wild geese travel south again."

The wheat has made a bitter crust
Seasoned with salt of many tears.
The bright leaves wither in the dust,
And wild geese call to deafened ears.

Though lips that spoke are silent now,
Love made recordings of the words
On wind and rain and leafy bough,
And songs of migratory birds.

ROBERT LEE BROTHERS

R. I. P.

Lo this man fought for God and right,
    And this for right and God;
They slew each other in one night
    And lie beneath the sod.

Here prostrate now they worship long
    The God whom all men trust,
And weigh uncertain right and wrong
    In scales of certain dust.

ARTHUR M. SAMPLEY

PASSOVER EVE

Beside his wife at Passover in spring
Jacob sits on pillows like a king.
Elijah may appear with flowing hair
To lift the dark and sing away despair.
That holy sage who utters truth in jest
May enter in the guise of unknown guest.
A cup of wine for him, and goblets too
Are set for absent ones. In sorrow's hue
Jacob, on such symbolic night of song,
Recalls his boys, slender and brave and strong.
His wife beholds the five dark handsome faces
Above the festive table's empty places.

As *Matzos* lie uneaten, candles sputter:
What says the wind that whispers in the shutter?

The mother speaks: *My prayer flies back and forth;*
Our boys lie east and west and south and north.
Each one has fallen in an alien land.
Prophet Elijah lift your holy hand
In succor . . . give us faith, dispel our fear
Our sons no longer sit beside us here.

Then suddenly the darkening shadow falls—
Upon the board, the floor, the dusky walls.
The Seder table lengthens and grows wide;
The sons come in and sit on either side;
The sons come in, as tall as pines are straight,
Elijah leading them. And from each plate
They lift the brimming goblets. Then like wind
Their voices echo, deep, yet strangely thinned:
"Forever keep the vow: That men be free
Like rain which gives sustenance to a tree,
That pestilence and sword be gone this hour;
The air be sweet with peace, the hedge in flower."

While Jacob chants the psalms, the candles sputter
And winds are whispering in every shutter.

FANIA KRUGER

ANSWER IN THE NIGHT

What is that noise in the street, Mother,
Has a new battle begun?
Hush, child! You must be dreaming,
The war is over and done.

But I can hear somebody weeping,
Why does it fill me with dread?
That is the cry of a starving child,
Freezing and begging for bread.

What was that flash on the skyline,
Why did the waves rise so high?
That was the test of an atom bomb,
Teaching a new way to die.

Why are the newspaper headlines
So big and black on the page?
The leaders are angry again today
And black is the mark of their rage.

Why should the leaders be angry,
Didn't the fighting cease?
Diplomats dare not agree, dear,
Each wants to dictate the peace.

Then whom must I hate next, Mother,
Russian or German or Pole?
Hate no man ever, my darling,
Hate is the death of the soul.

LEXIE DEAN ROBERTSON

221

MESSAGE FROM TUNISIA

If we who walk this flowering field with laughter
Should not tomorrow know the light of day,
If dawn should call, and we who followed after
Are silent and unheeding, then oh say
No bitter word of sorrow, no farewell
Laden with tears and restive in its grief;
Look on the dawn, you who with dawn may dwell,
And lift your singing hearts in bright belief.

Count not all lost because our day is gone.
Remember only that we too loved life
And for a while wooed beauty, sang with dawn,
And dared, though breath was sweet, to face the strife
That men hereafter might, as now we sing,
Greet dawn in freedom, know the peace of spring.

DAVID RUSSELL

PORTRAIT: AN AMERICAN VILLAGE

Quiet sleeps the village,
the women at their chores,
the old men all at labor,
the young men off to wars.

Quiet, quiet as the heart
in steady rhythm sure,
beneath the sleeping village
runs life that will endure.

No dream of slavery is there,
no pride of blood but this
calm pulse which takes all time
in quiet synthesis.

KEITH THOMAS

222

CHILDREN THROUGH WAR

Better than elders children may forget
and build in intervals their pleasant hours,
until the sirens and the bombs beset
their lives with strange, uncomprehended powers.

Again fantastic shapes of cloud resume
their Mother Goose procession down the skies,
and cease their function of a waiting room
from which, well-known, on many wings death flies.

Yet all the brilliant corridors down which
a child's dreams run like antelope and hare
are spotted now with shadow dark as pitch
and memory will hold the shadow there,
to be a scar, unmoved and undisplayed,
reminder of what new world must be made.

KEITH THOMAS

AT NIGHT'S BEGINNING

At night's beginning,
warmed and well fed,
I drew down the covers
of my smooth white bed.
Two blankets had I
woven deep
and a great woolen quilt
to muffle sleep.
I lay down softly
but I did not sleep.

I dialled the radio,
one, two, three,
and instantly tuned in
on agony.

The world grew so small
it came to rest
in the close cavern
of my breast.
It took my heart's place,
yet it could not rest,

but turned like a planet
to and fro
between its shadow
and the sun's great glow;
and the shadow's voice
was a voice of crying
as though children and old men
were slowly dying,
without enough breath
to be really crying.

The sound of hammers
rose and fell
where men chained together
were building hell;
and the vultures swung
from the sky in pity
where men stood penned
in a barbed wire city,
tended by men
who'd forgotten pity.

All this took place
in my own heart beat,
not far away
in time's dim street,
not in the pages
of history
but under the same sky
that sheltered me;
the same moon that saw this
shone on me.

And I cried when I saw
the shadow stand
upon the bright margin
of my land.
I cried to the world,
Oh world, stand still
lest the light be lost
from our field and hill.
But how could the heart
in my breast stand still?

Now half the world
was still bright as day.
The sun shone there
in its ancient way.
The fields stood green
and the trees bore fruit
and the red rose flowered
upon its root;
but why did man's own heart
bear no fruit?

For I saw man feeding
in gluttony
upon the bounty
of field and tree;
I saw man eating
the life of man.
Has this been so
since the world began?
Does man feast on the life
of his brother man?

And I saw I too
was nourished and fed
by the midnight tears
and the hearts that bled,
by pride gnawed close
on the bitten lip

and hatred that stung
like a salted whip
and love that had perished
in hunger's grip.

Man's sweat poured out
instead of mine
had fashioned my daily
bread and wine,
and the sheets I lay on
comfortably
were woven of all men's
agony
who had stooped in the fields
instead of me.

Women who stood
at the strident loom
were bound to me
in a single doom.
I was fed and eased
by their blood and breath.
I had gained my life
from their lives' slow death.
Must I not pay
with my living breath?

> "Cold wave in Europe"
>   the radio said,
> "The streets are wan
>   with the frozen dead."
> I pulled up the covers
>   over my head
> and tried not to hear
>   what the radio said;
> but I couldn't help hearing
>   what my own heart said.

PEGGY POND CHURCH

PART VIII

I Sing of Myself

The final section of SIGNATURE OF THE SUN is devoted to the personal lyric, poetry in which the identity of the poet dominates the world in which he writes. Originally, the term lyric was used to describe a poem composed to be sung, and accompanied by a lyre or Greek harp. As time went on, the use of the word broadened to include not only songs but all song-like poetry. Poems ranging all the way from songs in Shakespeare's plays to Wordsworth's "Ode on Intimations of Immortality" were classified as lyrics. When the distinctions between narrative and dramatic poetry came to be accepted, the degree of personal feeling and the simple declarative form came to differentiate lyric from non-lyric verse. There are lyrics in other sections of this book, but the majority of the poems asserting individual experience strongly, in the mood of a particular time or instance, have been placed here.

Each of the forty-four poets cannot be singled out for his individual lyric accent. The poems speak for themselves. But certain recognizable themes have helped the editors to plan the section. First, the poems on the seasons of the year. It is more than climate that calls forth poetry. Thermal changes produce a kind of climate of the mind, by which associations, auditory and visual images, memories are set forth in words. The seasons even have their rhythm, varying in subtleties which only the poetic mind can grasp. Transferred to listeners, other minds grasp them, too, and a meaning in nature is revealed. Karle Wilson Baker finds symbols of quiet and sustained love in "yellow leaves that whisper down" or in the "reticence of smoke." Early spring is more than the green dress of earth or robins to Haniel Long; it is the essential innocence that is both goodness and folly. To Reeve Spencer Kelley, spring is the web of growth, all merged into a tapestry of shapes, sights, and sounds. To Siddie Joe Johnson, Norman Macleod, Tom McNeal, Irene Carlisle, and the other poets here, man is like a magnetic field drawn to nature's center as the seasons pass. Yet within each man is a center, too, pulling nature to his own incentives and aspirations.

The poet and his calling are themes for Grace Noll Crowell, John McClure, Muna Lee, Ethel B. Cheney, Paul Eldridge, and Bertha Hart Nance, who say: "The poet finds a voice not only for himself, but for others as well. I bend my knee before my masters, Marlowe, Villon, Blake, and Shakespeare, and would burn my songs if I felt they were pretentious. It is hard to match the inexpressible with words. My poems are little houses on the sand, and yours are lovely rockbound mansions, secure above the lashings of the sea. Poets, beware of water—Shelley was drowned in the blue bay of Lerici. A mother reads her verses to me, while I look at two poems, her daughter and her son."

Some of the highest poetry in every form, narrative, dramatic, and lyric, has been proclaimed in the religious mood. A dozen Southwestern poets contribute to worship and awe through poetry before the shrines of morning and evening, hill and pine, God's quake and man's, the Messiah, the Holy Family, the human heart, the rhythm of life, the Spirit's light. As Whitman sang "of himself," he sang of all mankind, and of man's world, and of the Creator, as man could comprehend Him. Close to faith and its fruits in worship are the moments of contemplating self in the presence of all, man with his tick-tock of pulse before infinity. In such moments, every man is a poet. His decisions, both passive and active, spring from the inner spirit led by imagination. From the beginning of time, this spirit has been clouded, because men would not hear the poets. And at times the poets did not speak. "The darkening sight of men" will lift when the voice of the poet is a clear voice and when that voice is heard.

There is a poetry of accomplishment in the Southwest, as waste land has been reclaimed, as the wealth within the mountain and plain has been turned to human needs of both body and spirit. Perhaps the writers here have been less metaphysical than those in some literary areas, as they made use of poetry to describe the complexities of human experience; perhaps they have been less occupied with experiments in form. In the main, they have escaped the cultism and obscurantism which have divorced a good deal of modern poetry from a reading audience. Yet the editors believe that the poems in SIGNATURE OF THE SUN are contemporary in their approach to themes and modern in idiom and form. We leave this book with the reader in confidence that it has provided him with insight and refreshment.

I SHALL BE LOVED AS QUIET THINGS

I shall be loved as quiet things
Are loved—white pigeons in the sun,
Curled yellow leaves that whisper down
One after one;

The silver reticence of smoke
That tells no secret of its birth
Among the fiery agonies
That turn the earth;

Cloud-islands; reaching arms of trees;
The frayed and eager little moon
That strays unheeded through a high
Blue afternoon.

The thunder of my heart must go
Under the muffling of the dust—
As my grey dress has guarded it
The grasses must;

For it has hammered loud enough,
Clamored enough, when all is said:
Only its quiet part shall live
When I am dead.

KARLE WILSON BAKER

EARLY SPRING

Once more the prairie crocus
    Comes up beside the way;
The old earth has a green dress
    To put on to-day;

Children count the robins
    Along the road from school;
Again the sun is magic
    And I'm a fool.

HANIEL LONG

BUTTERFLIES

There will be butterflies,
There will be summer skies
    And flowers upthrust,
When all that Caesar bids
And all the pyramids
    Are dust.

There will be gaudy wings
Over the bones of things,
    And never grief:
Who says that summer skies,
Who says that butterflies,
    Are brief?

HANIEL LONG

SONG

Why should I have to take the highway
    When I can go through the wood:
What would be the use of it, what would be the fun,
    What would be the good?

Where I want to go the wood will take me,
    Its breath in my hands, in my hair;
Why should I hurry—isn't this much better
    Than getting somewhere?

HANIEL LONG

FOR REMEMBERING

Snows,
Hedges in rows,
And cars.
Skies behind limbs
Like bars.
Bridges like lattice,
Ridges like mounds;
Silence for hearing
Forgotten sounds.

REEVE SPENCER KELLEY

SEROUS SPRING

Spring is the fluid
    On newborn wings,
Wet on the web
    The spider strings;
Filament, damp,
    Of tawny grass
And weld of worms
    Beneath its mass;

        The tapioca
        Birth of frogs;
        And algae under
        Fallen logs;

The mist, the thick,
    The almost glue,
Deciding shape,
    And shade, and hue.

REEVE SPENCER KELLEY

THREE LEAVES FROM A TEXAS SUMMER

Summer, like an old mesquite,
Shook her branches over me;
I turned drowsy eyes to see
Line and contour of a tree;
On my face and on my eyes,
Three leaves fell and only three.

This is a new way the thicket has
Of wearing her green hair;
This is a new way the field has
Of looping the blue air.

This is a bright blue and a deep green
And a new road to follow;
Berries prickle the undergrowth;
Water lies in the hollow.

The first leaf fell
And, cool and thick,
I felt its comfort on my mouth.
Through its pulp, as through a wick,
Oil of life was warm and quick,
And June passed over the South.

Weeds, now, in the pastures,
And the sound of a grasshopper's wings.
The dry sound of the flight catches the throat;
The dry smell of the weeds clutches and stings.

Weeds, now, in the pastures—
Rag weeds higher than a young man's head.
This for a while is beauty's only drink;
This for a while is beauty's meager bread.

On my eyes I caught the press
Of the second leaf's caress.
Leather-hard and leather-thin,
Still it spoke of loveliness
And a pungent strength within.

Under the wind, the bones of the garden rattle;
Only a lizard springs from the burning ground;
Pomegranates hang and break in the withered hedges,
Spilling their rosy fruit without a sound.

Today a flock of blackbirds swooped in the sunlight
Making their wings a fantasy of shade.
The drouth moved backward a little, scenting autumn;
The heat stirred up from its sleep, caught and afraid.

Ultimate and brittle-brown,
The last leaf fell sharply down—
Fell and crumpled in its fall.
In a half a second's space,
It was dust upon my face,
And when I turned eyes to see
Leafy sorrow of a tree,
There was nothing over me—
There was nothing there at all.

SIDDIE JOE JOHNSON

QUICKENED EARTH

The seeds she planted hopefully
    Against an early spring,
Lift buds of sheer fragility
    For their brief blossoming.
The words she scattered with the seed,
    Against a later need,
In quickened earth have taken root,
    (Hush, my heart, your grieving)
And yield a firm and lasting fruit,
    Past all believing.

ISABEL HARRISS BARR

ULTIMATE WOUND

Beauty, strike deep
Into my spirit!
Let me keep
The hurt of your brand
In my hand.
Do not hide
The dull anguish
Of your striking;
Fling aside
The deceit
And the pretense, the fleet
Phrase, and the words
That seek to destroy.
Beauty, strike deep . . .
Then let me sleep,
Content
To have known
You.

ISABEL HARRISS BARR

YET AUTUMN MOURNFULLY

If flesh were only withered skin
Tented on my bones,
And hair a matted burlap-brown
Companion stones.

I would not hold with disregard
Fellowship and host
Who pattern chambers of the dead
More carelessly than most.

Cathedral dark, the desert caves
Moaning with the wind
Have seen what ages decompose
No silence will rescind.

Yet autumn mournfully will chant
Dirges that appeal
To hearts that may not cogitate
What senses may not feel.

NORMAN MACLEOD

RETURN IN OCTOBER

O, Boys and Girls, who walked the ways
    Where Plum Creek's bottoms dry and spread:
The land lies in October's haze,
    The trees are yellow and red—
    Can any more be said?

And on the edge of gathered fields
    The quails are calling in the grass,
And rabbits sit and take their meals,
    And all is as it was—
    Yes, everything, alas!—

Save now that boys who wear our eyes
And girls who wear our hair
Walk out beneath the Sunday skies
And speak each other fair——
Yet no one knows us there!

TOM H. McNEAL

THE MOMENT TREMBLES

The moment trembles on the leaf of time
Between dark certainty and unlikelihood;
And man is in that moment like a fawn
That waits the twig-snap in a winter wood,
While snows obliterate the hoof-worn trails
And make strange ghosts of all he understood;
Alert and tasting alien winds that blow
He strains to gather all a fawn can know.

FRANCES ALEXANDER

From AGAINST THE COLD

XX.

Autumn is only winter in disguise,
A mummer skeleton in scarlet cover.
Now is no spring nor summer in the skies,
But autumn comes and is a mortal mover.
Bones are the fingers now that touch the grass
And turn the edge of timothy and clover;
Bones are the feet that on the highway pass
And tread the weeds down and the gravel over.
So of adversity make stronger walls
Than stone or wood or clay or winds that hover

Along the meadowlands and waterfalls.
Be an amazed but undiscouraged lover
And build of better stuff than spring—the old
Unceasing fortitude against the cold.

WITTER BYNNER

WINTER WAKING

Shut in a silver room
We sigh and stir.
The wind is a wintry croon,
The earth a moving blur.

Morning cannot resume
The langorous sweep of night;
We are awake too soon
In the grey light.

Lie still in the huddled gloom;
The radiance is gone.
Love rose with the rising moon
And died at dawn.

IRENE CARLISLE

MELODY IN CRYSTAL

There was no sound on the frosty hill.
In a snowflake hush, all things were still.
The willow tree, that yesterday
Had hummed a madrigal of May,
Was quiet in a sheath of glass
Above the alabaster grass.

Then silver-bright, a melody
Ran tinkling through the crystal tree.
A singing, mutable and brief,
Awoke the grass and jeweled leaf.
And when the tune escaped the snare
Of stillness, I became aware
That silence, holding all spellbound,
Is the transparent source of sound.

RUTH AVERITTE

OTHER DAWNS

Against the east the blackness fades to gray.
    The dingy buildings bulk against the gloom,
And restlessly and faint and far away
    Life threads again the shuttles of its loom,
Weaving once more its web of mist and murk
    In grind of wheels and tread of passing feet.
The sparrows rouse—day's weariness and work
    Begins again along the clanging street—

Yet have I seen the day come swift and sweet;
    Yet have I seen the city tinged with fire
When gilded wall and tower rose to meet
    The rising sun with rapture and desire—
Old days, fair days that shall not come again—
    Yet still days come, and still the suns arise
And time and tide go on unchanged as when
    I watched dawn waken in thy dream-drugged eyes.

C. T. DAVIS

THE PIPER

We heard your sweet piping
Down in the hollow.
So, skipping and laughing,
We started to follow.
All our gay dimpled girls
And brave shouting boys
Deserted their playthings—
Their games and their toys.

We heard your pipes blowing
Over the hill.
But up at the summit
Your music was still.
You had vanished, O Piper!
So we climbed down again—
The bitter, old women
The gray, silent men.

ALICE BRILEY

AT WOODSTOCK

Lynx in the lilacs, dark as danger
Out of Asia; what is stranger

Than tropical cat that proudly stalks
Along these formal garden walks?

Hemmed by violet, hedged by rose
Softly the shining alien goes

Baffled by this cool flowered plot
Where mango and cinnamon trees are not.

Yet strange as panther in garden is,
There is a thing more strange than this.

Foreign as tiger must ever be
Scenting hawthorn; wondrously

Like to a leopard in green lands,
Removed from all he understands,

Is love, bright beast, amazed to find
Himself in the austere, ordered mind.

FRANCES RANSON

UPON THIS MOUNT

The instrument, the chart
But serve the questing art.
Alone, it marks the star,
Lucid, particular;
In all the glistered bowl
Seeks out the fleck, sharp, sole—
Plucks from the pail of space
Keen grain, the splendid trace.

For Man himself's the mirror
Brings knowledge any nearer;
The hollow of his dream
Divines that mighty stream
So even what is errant
Shows truth the more apparent:
Where we misapprehend
Error begins to end.

Upon this faith's strong mount
Take confident account:
Earth's tilt, and turn of night,
Year's curve, the zenith's height—
Of every variable
Compound new miracle.
See with the staring mind
Before the eye shall find.

Who shall distinguish what
Unplotted Ultimate
Burns in the watcher's scope,
Climbs the galactic slope?
The mind, the heart, the soul
All are one fertile Whole
That ever outward moves
Conceiving as it proves.

WILLIAM BARNEY

HALF-BRACELET

I have a broken piece of silver in my hand
Remembering you beside me on the sand
Of a river bank, lying in the sun
And bending (as the Indian might have done
Who made the bracelet, but this time to break)
A circlet which a silversmith had worked to make.

I hold the twisted strand and treasure more
The troubled hands that broke it on the shore
Than any other hand or other wrist
That either I or bracelets ever kissed . . .

WILLARD "SPUD" JOHNSON

MOUNTAIN PARTING

We have travelled awhile together—
A desert, a mountain, a year;
And you are as young as a Chinese hill,
And I as old as fear . . .

Tomorrow we shall be parting,
In a month, or maybe a week;
Between us, like Yi and his brother,
Will be "autumn, peak after peak."

WILLARD "SPUD" JOHNSON

GIFTS

I freely give you everything:
The deeds I do, the songs I sing,
My wisdom and my discontent,
My restlessness, my merriment,
My strength, my weakness and my tears,
The foibles of my thirty years.

I give you all the dreams I've dreamed,
My heart where love's bright fire has gleamed,
The magic of the spring, my youth,
What little I have found of truth,
The thread of hope that yet remains,
The new delights, the old refrains.

And in return I ask no boon,
For bargains are but ashes soon;
Your satisfaction, thanks, your kiss
To me are but a moment's bliss.
My more enduring thanks will be
That you accept these gifts of me!

DAVID RUSSELL

WONDER

If radio's long hands
Can pluck voices from a world of night
And bear them over continents
And seas to me—
Bring echoes of wild joy
From distant cities
To this lonely room of mine
And drop them at my feet
As naturally as a crimson rose
Drops from the dying bush,
Surely, sometime, somewhere
I shall be able to catch
The echo of your voice
Again!

BYRON CHEW

THE HOME-COMING

Forget the moon, forget the lift of stars
    Over dark trees, over the glistening lake;
Under them shadow and moonbeam rumor old wars
    Down the path that I must take.

Here long ago it was—too long for tears,
    Almost too long for the heart's remembering—
My mother walked with me through boyhood years,
    Under the stars of spring.

Fireflies wake in the wood a golden spark;
    The world is behind me now, I must go alone,
Led by her quiet shadow from dark to dark,
    With a heart heavy as stone.

I must go back a path where no path is,
    And search for her young face, I know not where,

Touch her cool hand, turn from her parting kiss,
  And leave her forever there.

High in the summer stars her pale brow gleams,
  Legend or myth that haunts me near and far.
I must wander alone tonight a path of dreams,
  Led by a vanished star.

PATRICK DACUS MORELAND

From I KNOW TWO MEN

1.

My father is a farmer,
  Righteous and good;
He plows as straight a furrow
  As any man could.

My sweetheart is a poet:
  Every line goes
Straight as an arrow,
  Like my father's rows.

2.

My father loves the land,
  My sweetheart, the sky;
And so, half-orphaned,
  Half-widowed am I;

For I love the ocean,
  As Neptune's daughter;
I know my father only
  Where land touches water.

I know my lover only
  Where the sea meets the sky,
And so, half-widowed,
  Half-orphaned am I.

VAIDA STEWART MONTGOMERY

NOT TOO FAR

I'd be sea-foam or wood smoke,
or, if I thought it would please,
I'd be rain at a cabin window——
though I am none of these.

The thundering bolt of words
when your heart is a shaken storm,
or a stubborn bit of earth
for your restless fingers to form.

Since little lives are so mortgaged
and it seems I'll be busy elsewhere,
I would be, in your hands, cupped water,
or sunlight on your hair.

O I would, if I could, be always
whether blueberry, cricket, or star,
alive . . . somewhere . . . for you
and not too far.

MARCELLE CHANCELLOR LEATH

TO CERTAIN CURIOUS

O strip my pride like an apple pared,
or prick my peace like the thistle,
but never ask me how I fared
when I caught Love's lilting whistle.

O squirm me under your microscope
—a bitter branch has a reason——
ask what winds have withered hope
but not of Love's green season.

For there blossoms here what's overdue
—there's the smell of late rains pouring—
and you might catch my eyes on you
    naked and adoring.

MARCELLE CHANCELLOR LEATH

From LADY OF APRIL

Nine love sonnets

II.
I had rebuked myself most reverendly
And said: "Tut! Let love vanish!" I had said:
"Love is a madness, an insanity.
Forget it wholly." Now, discomfited,
I wonder how it came about at all
That I forgot all learning and all sense
And fell a-laughing and grew musical,
Loving you gaily, with no recompense.
"Tut! Let love vanish?" Faith, I will, my dear,
Let this love vanish, and with little care,
In the august apocalyptic year
When earth and ocean vanish into air.
"Tut! Let love vanish!" said I? Faith, I will
When stars are ashes and the suns stand still.

JOHN McCLURE

ALTAR CANDLES

The yuccas flowering proudly
    Beside the garden wall
Are white cathedral candles,
    Waxen and stately-tall.

MARY ANNE DAVIS

THE FIRST NIGHT

This is his first night in the grave,
    And oh, he loved the light.
I cannot bear to think of him
    With shrouded sight.

This is his first night in the grave,
    And oh, he loved the air.
I cannot breathe when I think of him
    As stifled there.

This is his first night in the grave,
    Goodbye, my dearest Dear.
Will it comfort you to know that I
    Shall soon sleep near?

MARY ANNE DAVIS

THE POET

Out of the highest agonies of pain;
Out of the holiest sorrows he must come;
From passion unto passion he must gain
The heights beyond the heights—and standing dumb
Within the awful silence of the past,
Burst into song—so winged with flame—so free—
That every tired heart will say: "At last—
Some one has found my voice—and sings for me."

GRACE NOLL CROWELL

248

APOLOGY

I am a poetaster
    And my knee I bend
To Marlowe, my master,
    Villon, my friend.

I am a swashbuckler,
    And I break my sword
Before Blake, my tutor,
    Shakespeare, my lord.

I should burn my song-books
    This very day
If singing didn't matter
    So little anyway.

JOHN McCLURE

OF WRITING VERSE

When the granite mountain wavers into shadow,
    Or streams like a banner on the sky;
When the green corn tossing makes an ocean of the
        meadow,
    Or a night of blackbirds rushes by:

It is hard to watch the subtle changes of the mountain
    Or hear the exultation of the birds,
And stubbornly to grip the patient pen between my fingers
    Setting down my littleness in words.

MUNA LEE

TO A GREATER POET

My poems are little houses on the sand.
From their small windows I look longingly
To where your lovely rockbound mansions stand,
Secure above the lashings of the sea.

I look upon tall pillars beauty twined
With old time ivy that is ever green;
Upon your gracious windows that are lined
Against the shadows gathering between.

I look upon your many gardens fair,
And in my heart is joy with pain beside.
Your mansions stand, but soon the waves will bear
My broken houses out upon the tide.

ETHEL B. CHENEY

A WARNING TO POETS

I.

Poets, beware of water—
Shelley was drowned in the blue bay of Lerici;
A volume of Keats was in his hand.
It was opened.
A volume of Sophocles was in his pocket.
And they were drowned—
All three were drowned
In that bright blue bay.

II.

Down in the Creek Nation
Near Eufaula,
In the green placid water of the Oktahutchee river,
Alexander Posey, the Creek poet,
Was drowned in a few feet of water,
The canoe was drifting—and the nature-lover
Had communed the last time

With the sleek, lovely water-moccasins
And the bright green turtles,
When his wife found that empty shell,
The canoe.

III.

I knew a boy, an Indian boy—
He was a dancer;
He could touch the ground with his shoulder
And the back of his head
In the Sac and Fox dances.
Once in Chilocco he picked up in his mouth
Three eagle feathers he had stuck in the ground,
As the crowd watched him
Posturing, stamping, writhing.
He was a poet—
And he was drowned when the water of Deep Fork
Sucked up through the ice and reached hungrily
For him skating there on its surface,
And engulfed him, its wished-for prey,
With a rhythm as imperious as his own . . .

Poets, beware of water—
Shelley was drowned in the blue bay of Lerici,
A book of Keats in his hand,
A volume of Sophocles in his pocket.

PAUL ELDRIDGE

POET MOTHER

One spicy winter evening
She read to me her verse,
And some of it was better,
And some of it was worse.

The while they sat and watched us
With glances deep and long,
Her boy, who is a sonnet,
Her girl, who is a song.

She is a skillful rhymer,
Her lines are neatly done,
Two poems I remember,—
The daughter and the son.

BERTA HART NANCE

LITANY FOR NEW MEXICO

Bless God for the day!

Bless Him for the wide clear-flowing
New Mexico morning,
Poured round the shadow pools,
Gilt on the cumbres.

Bless Him for the nooning,
When the white thunderheads with sails full bowing
Sleep on the three wind rivers.
Bless God and praise Him
For the west-sloping hour of siesta
Under domed cottonwoods,
That in a rainless land make ever the sound of rain.

Bless Him for the evening;
For the releasing cool hands of the wind
On the flushed headlands;
For the lilac and larkspur veils
Let down by the mothering mountains
Between the work that fails and the dream that lingers.
Bless Him for home-coming sounds—
The window-shine on the loma,
For the welcoming flame and the savory smell
And the snuggling cry of the children.

Bless God for the night!
Bless him for the keen curled sickle that reaps
The saffron meadows of the sun's late sowing;

For the full-shaped globe of wonder,
Pacing the eastern ranges.
Oh, bless Him more than all
For the ever-recurrent orb that emerges
Between the light that goes and earth's oncoming shadow.

Bless Him for shared sleep,
For the midnight's healing fountain,
For the companionable cock-crow, warning
The sleeper back from dreams to the pastures of morning.

Bless God for the dawning,
For the earth collecting
Darkness again to her breast,
For the hills resounding
Clarion blue to the sun's relucence.

Bless God and praise Him
With exceeding thanksgiving
For His gift of the day and the night!

MARY AUSTIN

EVE OF CHAOS

At every compasspoint the seismographic needles wheeled
To diagram a quake.
We caused that tremor; weeping we fell upon the ground
        in an anguish
That made the earth shake.

And now we cry a warning to the ancient god
To look to his faltering star,
Lest in a greater fear we shatter it wholly with none to
        witness
Where any fragments are.

GRACE ROSS

STORM AT NIGHT

The wind came hurdling out of space
And drove rain-javelins in my face:

A thousand cannons rent the air,
And zigzag lightning singed my hair,

And save for it I could not see
A single step ahead of me,

Yet down the uncertain road I trod,
Very intimate with God.

WHITNEY MONTGOMERY

MESSIAH

Has the Messiah come?
Or is He the ever-coming?
Racing with clouds, a light against shadow,
Or as the sun turning the night into dawn,
To be lost again in darkness?

What is a Messiah?
A word of peace to scatter the gloom of war?
Youth with its dreams and yearning,
Flowering into manhood,
To old age, and then once more into youth?

Is he a child conceived in love?
A wave upon the widening sea?
A star at twilight?
The struggle, the groping and climbing to the crest
of a hill?

The oak from the acorn?
Life from death?

Has the Messiah come?
Or is He the ever-hoped for, the ever-coming?

FANIA KRUGER

IF I HAD BEEN IN BETHLEHEM

Could I have been in Bethlehem
The night that Jesus came,
There in that simple manger room
While angels sang acclaim,

Where patient cattle stood amazed
Deep in the fragrant straw,
And humble shepherds quietly knelt
With reverence and awe,

I would have knelt and prayed with them,
But I know all the while
My eyes would look where Mary sat
To see her tender smile,

To watch the glow that lit her face
With radiance that none
Has ever known but mothers who
Caress a first-born son.

I would have found eternal light
Beside that sacred flame,
Could I have been in Bethlehem
The night that Jesus came.

LEXIE DEAN ROBERTSON

THE HUMAN HEART

This intricate machine within the breast,
Set there to run untouched from birth to death—
I marvel at a thing that knows no rest
By day or night as long as there is breath.
God made a million things: the moon, the sun,
He flung the planets and the stars apart,
Created seas and mountains, and this done,
Set at His master-task: the human heart.

A living, pulsing, wild tempestuous thing
That joy would lift, and sorrow would cast down;
Where faith would dwell, and hope and laughter spring;
Where Love would have its kingdom and its crown.
I think God must have waited—awed to start
The mechanism of the human heart.

GRACE NOLL CROWELL

THE UNBROKEN RHYTHM

Perhaps we shall find at last that life and death
Are part of the same poem, rhyme on rhyme,
With but a natural pausing for the breath
As a sentence ends; that swinging out from time
Into eternity will make no break at all;
That still the perfect rhythm will be there;
That the singing, high, sustained notes will not fall,
Nor the music falter on the waiting air.

I trust that there will be no stumbling feet
To mar the progress of that perfect thing.
The epic we call "life" is strangely sweet,
And yet, God grant upon its upward swing
It may take on, beneath an abler hand,
A meaning that the heart can understand.

GRACE NOLL CROWELL

LITANY

Moon filling the night with green,
Suckle the mesa, flat and lean.

Ave Maria, Madre de Dios.

Candles holding my body so still,
Guide the traveler over the hill.

Ave Maria, Madre de Dios

Flowers my hands now cherishing,
Come back without me in early spring.

Ave Maria, Madre de Dios.

Tears over me so silently shedding,
Flow again brightly at the next wedding.

Ave Maria, Madre de Dios

Son, sitting quietly here by my side,
Go forth tomorrow with Joy for your bride.

Ave Maria, Madre de Dios.

PAUL HORGAN

MARY

Miriam, Mary, Maria, Marie
What voweled jewel might this be?

Is it a sapphire, love,
Of purest water true?
Or is it water of
A sapphire hue?

Miriam, Marie, Maria, Mary,
So crystal-cut, yet limpid airy!

It flows in regal tones,
Glitters like both of these:
The sea-reflecting stones,
The jeweled seas.

Mary, Marie, Maria, Miriam,
Ocean of beryl, sea-lit beryllium!

Gem for the Father's ring,
Stone of the Son's great crown,
Glint on the Spirit's wing,
Light pouring down.

Miriam, Mary, Marie, Maria,
Pendant for my lips, Maria!

FRAY ANGELICO CHAVEZ

SHADOWS

Mary, as upon your breast
Lay our little Lord at rest,
Did you see, in terror dread,
Shades of thorn about His head?

Mary, as you sang your psalms,
As you kissed His rosy palms,
Did the shadow of a scar
Sometimes their perfection mar?

Mary, as He gravely played
Underneath the olive-shade,
Did your eyes, tear-misted, see
The shadow of another tree?
*   *   *

God is good, and God is kind,
That He makes all mothers blind!

GOLDIE CAPERS SMITH

SHINING TRAILS

Mary's path from Elizabeth's house;
    The Wise Men's star-lit way;
The Apostles' road from Olivet;
    The way Paul went, for prey;
Each was and is a shining trail
    Bright with a heavenly ray.

The blood-wet paths of martyrdom;
    The routes Crusaders found;
Young Joan's road to Orleans;
    Columbus' way, west-bound;
Each was a trail that shone with light,
    Rugged but glory-crowned.

The wake (to a rover) of outbound ships;
    The church aisle, to a bride;
The gleaming rails that worldward stretch,
    To bright youth village-tied;
They are shining trails to eager feet
    And hearts unsatisfied.

And poems like little trails are found
    That catch a wanderer's sight,
Lure from the valley's narrow bound
    And struggle toward the height,
Leading aloft where all the ground
    Shines with the Spirit's light.

CLYDE WALTON HILL

A PAGAN MOOD

World, go worship as you will:
I am but a pagan still.

You may mouth your little creeds,
Chant your anthems, count your beads,

Underneath your temple's roof:
I, from town and spires aloof,

Just for one soft Sabbath day
Worship in the ancient way.

Gone the shrines of pagan folk,
Blown the sacrificial smoke,

But a sentient something clings
Of the old imaginings,

So that sward and sky for me
Wear the guise of deity;

Hoary hill and rugged pine
Own a majesty divine,

And in shadows soft and dim,
Lo, I bow and worship them!

HILTON ROSS GREER

PLACE FLINT STONES AT MY ROOTS

Place flint stones at my roots,
Roof down my head,
But never, NEVER say
That I am dead!

Place me in a dungeon!
I know the sky—
I shall not bow my head.
Not I—Not I!

Tie me in a coffin.
Clamp the hinges tight.
I shall rise again
And find the light—

ROSA ZAGNONI MARINONI

NUMERATOR

When I lived in the country
    Near half a dozen men,
I thought the earthly universe,
    Divisible by ten.

When I moved to the village
    Among a hundred score,
My fraction grew much smaller,
    Its denominator more.

When I came to the city
    Where thousands walked the street
My portion of the universe
    Was that beneath my feet.

When I became a traveller
    And saw the strangers throng,
I knew my ego fraction
    Was still a little wrong.

My share kept growing smaller
    At every port of call
Until the numerator me
    Seemed scarcely there at all.

FRANCES ALEXANDER

STAMPEDE

My thoughts, like cattle, roam the pastures of my mind.
Some plod along the beaten paths
Like my father's white-faces,
Content to munch their measured portions,
And drink from wooden tanks,
And browse around familiar places,
And lie heavily at night,
Unruminant.

But there are some like mavericks,
A motley herd, strayed from a thousand flocks,
As if they had been rounded-up
From passing generations
Unbranded.
They mill around restlessly
Dreaming of fenceless prairies
And of needle-grass oceans
Billowing endlessly;
They sniff for the scent of cacti blossoms
Riding the western breeze
And search for the dancing shadows
Of lace-leafed mesquite trees.

They want to feel the prick of thorns
Upon their tongues,
And to lick white salt from huge rocks
Pallid in the sun.
They long to stand upon the canyon's brink
Where varicolored walls
Mar Nature's face with many livid scars,
Or to drink from the shallow bed of a river
Where the ever-shifting quicksands quiver.
At night when they lie bedded down
It is not to sleep,
But to listen for ancient terrors that may creep in
To haunt their timid souls.
The teeth of a blizzard may pierce deep

Or a hungry beast may prowl,
Or that unseen, unknown, nameless thing
May stalk into their midst.

O, night-guards, as you make your rounds tonight
Keep careful watch;
Croon softest lullabies to soothe this restless herd to sleep.
Some fancied enemy, even a rolling weed,
May sweep these wanderers from ancestral ages
Into terrified
Stampede.

VAIDA STEWART MONTGOMERY

INCOMPREHENSION

No day goes by but what I find
The spikes of wonder pierce my mind;
So varied is the day's expanse
I feed upon sharp wonder's lance.

How any man alive can be
Unshaken by immensity,
Or walk unheedful of the bright
Cascade of beauty-laden light,

Or miss the stinging arrows of
The manifold designs of love
That weave through every living thing
And make the shining moments sing,

How any man alive can find
The path of living dull and blind
While spears of wonder pierce and rend,
Is more than I can comprehend!

DAVID RUSSELL

BIRDS

The world's a tree where birds abide,
Varied in kind from hawk to dove,
And some fly high, and some wing wide,
In quest of food for hate or love
Unsatisfied.

Fierce beauty rides the falcon's flight
To stalk fair beauty for a prey
In wooing wood-doves bred in fright;
The swallows streak the day with grey
As meteors the night with light;
And ghastly grand the gliding way
Of carrion-kite.

A bird I know looked far beyond
Such flights for beauty's lasting fruit
That must lie past the loftiest frond,
Much farther than the deepest root,
And yet is reached and held in bond
Without pursuit.

At last he found himself a cage,
Not out of fear of loves and wars
That make some seek a hermitage;
Within a doorless cage with bars
He chose to live more staid and sage
To reach for stars.
The open cage swings from the tree
Where all his fellows fly and feed;
The caged bird sings in it and free
Filling, unfilled, its only need
For mystery.

He reaches for bread upon the moon
Between the bars or through the door;
Pecks sparkling star-seed heaven-strewn
Upon the night-reflecting floor,
Or sips the mirrored blue of noon,
A-thirst for more.

Comes Time the Huntsman to ensnare,
Chasing to weary wings the fleet,
But spares the captive of such care;
He scares from field and flesh their meat,
But his stays there.

Someday will Time stop short and thrust
His ruthless hand into the cage;
The bird will die as dreamers must,
But not by any arrow of age:
Whose fare knew neither worm nor rust
Is phoenix dust,
Latent-lit to rise like One,
Clothed with the sun.

FRAY ANGELICO CHAVEZ

IN THE HARVEST

The sun shines hot from a clear sky.
I laugh and lay my pitchfork by.
Why work for food and drink and bed
When one has dreams within one's head?
In this world it is best to sit
In silence and consider it.
Ay, while the slipshod minutes flee,
This is the sweetest work for me,
To lie a-dreaming dreamily
And watch great God Almighty's fleet
Drive slowly over the fields of wheat—
With a salt sea-song in my throat
Lie belly-upward, taking note
How solemnly go by
Those galleys of the sky.

The little ants among the grass
Upon their daily routine pass.
The farmer lads make the wheat fly.

Say, do I envy them? Not I.
The horses that the reaper pull
Know not the world is beautiful.

I watch the great white clouds go by
Like ships across the open sky
Until a magic memory
Of sounding surge comes back to me,
And here, forgetful of it all—
The busy men, the farmer's call—
I lie a-dreaming dreamily
About the sea-gulls and the sea.

JOHN McCLURE

MY SINS AND I

I took my little secret sins
Down to the creek to drown,
Five cunning ones of black and white
And two of shining brown.

I set them down in one long row
And bade them meditate
Upon their foolish wicked ways
That led them to this fate.

They looked at me so wistfully
And promised to be good;
I yielded to their pleading eyes
And hid them in the wood.

But when I had reached home again,
There, perched upon my sill,
Were all those naughty sins of mine,
And they are with me still!

LEXIE DEAN ROBERTSON

I LOVE THIS LITTLE TOWN

I love this little town that has grown up
With me, I love the way this quiet street
Runs softly down its locust lane to meet
The country fields, and when the locusts cup
Their slender, plumed hands the more to hold
Their brimming nectar, all the streets throw wide
Their doors and lilies burn their lamps of gold
Along the garden paths—bright lamps to guide

The children's feet—oh then this little town
Is lovely! All the drab, familiar things
Are new with sudden glamour, murmurings
Of laden bees attune the day, and drown
The voice of Care, while mocking birds—but stay—
Who would not love this little town in May?

DAISY LEMON COLDIRON

TEACHER

You wonder if my task grows old to me.
If telling many times has not made stale
The stories that illumine history:
Of one whose gallant heart had faith to sail
Upon a turbulent, unfathomed sea;
Of him who bore the name of Nathan Hale;
Of her who caught a gleam at Domremy
Which filled her with a light that could not fail.

Then I recall a youth who, eager-eyed,
Listened one day with face like Israfil,
And walked as if a sword hung by his side,
—In France, a white cross blossoms on a hill.
Yes, teaching is sometimes a weary task;
Sometimes, the holiest mission one may ask.

GOLDIE CAPERS SMITH

OF THOSE WHO WORE THE WOUND INSIDE

Of those who wore the wound inside
And died of ills they never knew,
Concealing from the inward view
The cancer that they could not hide,

Of those who looked into the glass
And saw the man they did not see
And wondered how the world could be
So heedless as to let him pass,

Of those who, walking in the sun,
Have cast no shadows, I was one.

ARTHUR M. SAMPLEY

BOX-CAR LETTERS

Alone on the hill where the sun goes down
I plunder the earth from my little town;
But the spoils I bring in my fairy sack
Are scattered and spilled on the railroad track . . .
For there, on the siding, the box-cars doze,
And this is the way their dreaming goes:

"Sault Sainte-Marie and Chicopee,
Miami and San Antonio—"
They call like a lover's song to me,
Call, and I want to go!
Santa Fé, Norfolk and Kalamazoo,
Sacramento, Mobile, Peru—
How, do you think, you could tamely bide
In the one small spot where your heart was tied,
When those haughty drudges came creaking through,
Tearing your anchored heart in two,

Each with a name on its solid side
Two feet tall and ten feet wide,
That rings like a chime for you?

The wanderer's day will have one good hour,
And every roadside one magic flower;
They wither and droop if you stay too long,
The perfume goes like an ended song.
I would come back to the ways I know
But I would not stay when I want to go!

Wichita, Bangor, and San José,
Ypsilanti and Monterey—
They flutter my peace like the tang of spray!
From high dream-pastures homing down
To the fold of my heart in the little town,
I have to wait at the railroad track
On a trundling train with a snorting stack!
The engine's a genie, a grimy scamp
Who turns a philosopher into a tramp.
Denver, Seattle and Calumet,
Natchez, New Haven and Laramie—
Go on with your lumbering lure, and let
A poor philosopher be!

KARLE WILSON BAKER

I REMEMBER

My father rode a horse
        And carried a gun;
He swapped for a living
        And fought for his fun—
I remember his spurs
        A-gleam in the sun.

My father was always
     Going somewhere—
To rodeo, market,
     Or cattleman's fair—
I remember my mother,
     Her hand in the air.

FAY M. YAUGER

HERITAGE

My father was tall as a tree is tall
     And straight as a tree is straight,
A man who was sudden in ways of love
     And sudden, as well, in hate.

My mother was tiny and somber-eyed,
     Vague as a shadowed pool:
Chary of words and chary of smiles,
     Cool as the rain is cool.

My father craved, as all bold men do,
     Such errands as tried his might:
A horse to break, or a man to fist,
     Or a wrong to set aright.

My mother craved, as most women do,
     A chimney to call her own,
An acre of land, a team in the stall,
     A pot on the warming-stone.

My father wandered, as such men must,
     She followed as women will,
And I was born with my face to the sky,
     My shoulders against a hill.

And I am sudden in love and hate
    (This to my father's pride)
But I am small, as my mother was,
    And I am somber-eyed.

And I am marked by a double need
    That's bred in the flesh and bone:
For roads that climb to the high hill's top,
    And a chimney to call my own.

FAY M. YAUGER

EPHEMERIDES

    Upon receiving from an Arizona friend a letter which contained this paragraph:

A voice spoke in a vivid dream, saying, 'But what you must know is—Ariel died yesterday—no fuss; simply; suddenly Ariel was not; and now I can never—'

    Ariel died the other night?
And was he not your close-attending sprite,
Your merry-andrew, rogue, and servitor
Who breathed a whiff of England and Romance
Upon the hills where you are sorcerer
    By unaccountable mischance,
    Lord over cactus and mesquite,
Lord over all—but stalking, snarling heat?

    You were his second Prospero,
From whom he never wheedled leave to go
Away, away, freed from your sure command.
The slave pitied the master. In your smile
He found a sorrow that was contraband;
    Mindful he was, and wise, the while
    To bring you sprigs of jessamine,
The wild crab apple, and a winking wine.

Ariel was not meant to die
Except beneath a spring-blue English sky.
That he who was the heart of fairy lore
In desert waste or meadow, ever humming
A gay midsummer tune, should be no more!
    To wait expectant for his coming,
    To find him riding up the road,
The saucy one, perched on a horned toad!

    Make a bold pretense of it
And conjure Hope, the almost hypocrite,
To be your helot. Tell no more, except
With laughter on your tongue, as in a dream;
For counsel lightly told is counsel kept,
    And that is far the sager scheme.
    What will become of Prospero
With Ariel gone? Only the morrows know.

                                EDWARD DORO

PRAYER

        Let us not look upon
        Their like again,
        This generation
        Of bewildered men,—
        With earth-roads, sea-roads,
        Sky-roads too, that show
        All ways to enter
        And no way to go.

                        WITTER BYNNER

272

TAKE AWAY THE DARKNESS

Against the sun there sets a moon.
Against the moon a sun.
Is it the west begun too soon,
Or the east too late begun?

All that I know or ever knew
Is that I began in space
And for a while I come and go
With light upon my face.

And darkness is as good as light
While both shall be again—
Except the darkening of sight
Made by the might of men.

WITTER BYNNER

Acknowledgments

Acknowledgment and appreciation are hereby given to the following poets, publishers, and periodicals for permission to use poetry appearing in SIGNATURE OF THE SUN.

To authors holding copyrights, as follows: Lou Ellen Archer, "Monument Valley," *Sonnets to the Southwest;* Carlos C. Ashley, "The Sheriff's Widow," *That Spotted Sow;* Ruth Averitte, "A Prairie Boy's Need," *Cowboy Over Kiska;* "Melody in Crystal," which appeared in *Adventures in Poetry* (1946), edited by Ted Malone; Stanley E. Babb, "High Noon—Galveston Beach," "Portrait of a Pirate," *The Death of a Buccaneer;* Karle Wilson Baker, "Box-Car Letters," "Good Company," "I Shall Be Loved as Quiet Things," "Song of the Forerunners," *Dreamers on Horseback;* W. E. Bard, "San Luis Pass," "To a Skyscraper," *A Little Flame Blown;* S. Omar Barker, "New Mexico," *Vientos de las Sierras,* "When Billy the Kid Rides Again," *The Golden Stallion* (1930), edited by D. Maitland Bushby; Lena Whitaker Blakeney (for Harold Vinal, Publisher), "Nouveau Riche," *Ports of Call;* Margie B. Boswell, "The Texas Ranger," A. L. Crouch, "Ben Milam," Grace Ross, "Eve of Chaos," Margaret Fox Thompson, "Furlough," "Study in Metal," *Out Where the West Begins* (1949), edited by Grace Ross and Mabel M. Kuykendall; Alice Briley, "The Piper"; Fray Angelico Chavez, "Birds," "Peña Blanca," *Clothed with the Sun;* Byron Chew, "Give Me the Apples," *Thumbprints;* Peggy Pond Church, "At Night's Beginning," *Ultimatum for Man;* A. L. Crouch, "Sentry," *This Is Really Living;* Reid Crowell, "Old Plaza in Albuquerque," *The Old Intensities;* Katherine A. Murdock Davis and the Bar D Press, Siloam Springs, Arkansas, for her poem, "The Little Town," from *The Broken Necklace,* and for "Altar Candles," "The First Night," and "The Trees of Fayetteville," by Mary Anne Davis, from *From My Window;* Glenn Ward Dresbach, "In the Desert," "The Needle's Eye," *In Colors of the West,* "The Fence," *Cliff Dwellings and Other Poems,* "The Water Finder," *The Enchanted Mesa;* Paul R. Eldridge, "Grey Roadster," "A Warning to Poets"; Everett A. Gillis, "Hello the House," "Letter to the People," *Hello the House;* Imogene P. Greer, for poems by her husband, Hilton Ross Greer, "To a Bird on a Down Town Wire," "The Road of Midnight

Pageants," "A Pagan Mood," *Ten and Twenty Aprils;* Louise Cram Hill, for a poem by her husband, Clyde Walton Hill, "Shining Trails," *Shining Trails;* Vera Holding, "Prairie Brand," *Prairie Brand,* "Sand Storm," "Tornado," *Prairie Nautilus;* Boyce House, "Beauty Is Elsewhere," "Cities," *Texas Rhythm;* Margaret Bell Houston, "Song From Traffic," *The Singing Heart and Other Poems;* Siddie Joe Johnson, "Sea-Hunger," "Three Leaves From a Texas Summer," *Agarita Berry;* Spud Johnson, "Half-Bracelet," "Mountain Parting," "Yellow," *Horizontal Yellow;* Farona Konopak, "Truchas," *Adobe in Sunlight;* Marcelle Chancellor Leath, "The Long Night," "Not Too Far," "To a Certain Curious," *Awake in the Night;* Muna Lee, "Of Writing Verse," *Sea Change;* Therese Lindsay, "Bluebonnets," Grace Ross, "Poor White Sketch," *Texas Poems* (1936), edited by Vaida S. Montgomery; Haniel Long, "Indians," from *The Midland,* "Butterflies," "Early Spring," "Song," *Atlantides;* Lilith Lorraine, "To Will Rogers and Wiley Post," *Let the Patterns Break;* Lilith Lorraine, "Southwest," Berta Hart Nance, "Texan," Nancy Richey Ranson, "San Jacinto Battlefield," Goldie Capers Smith, "Alamo," *The Road to Texas* (1940), edited by Whitney Montgomery; Norman Macleod, "Santo Domingo," *We Thank You All the Time,* "Hotevilla," "Yet Autumn Mournfully," *The Golden Stallion,* ed. Bushby; Berta Hart Nance, "Carlsbad Cave," "Cattle," *Flute in the Distance,* "Lines From Arizona," "Poet Mother," *Lines from Arizona;* Richard Leon Spain, "The Hangar," "Hill Farmer's Epitaph," *Rock and Cumulus;* Herbert Joseph Spinden, "Song of the Sky Loom," *Songs of the Tewa;* Helen D. Stevens, for a poem by her husband, Thomas Wood Stevens, "Coronado Came on Horseback," *Westward Under Vega;* Alan Swallow, "To My Infant Daughter," *The War Poems of Alan Swallow;* Annette Hesch Thorp, for poems collected by her husband, N. Howard (Jack) Thorp, and for "Little Joe the Wrangler," which he wrote; Zoe A. Tilghman, "Cowboy, Cowboy!" "Healing," *Prairie Winds.* To authors permitting us to print uncopyrighted material: Alice Gill Benton, "Samurai"; George Bond, "In Winter" and "In Early Spring"; Carey Holbrook, "Little Houses," from *Life Goes On;* Charles Wiley, "The White Beneath."

To Vaida and Whitney Montgomery of *Kaleidograph* Magazine for generously supplying information about poets and for permissions granted through Kaleidograph Press, Dallas, as follows: Walter R. Adams, "Cotton," from *The Dead Lie Down;* Frances

Alexander, "Numerator," "The Moment Trembles," from *Time at the Window;* John Houghton Allen, "If I Had Never Dreamed of Poetry," "There Is Something About the Brush," from *Song to Randado;* Robert Lee Brothers, "Forces," "Raindrop," "War and the Farmer Boy," from *Democracy of Dust;* Daisy Lemon Coldiron, "Desert Gods," "Quanah Hears Two Calls," from *Songs of Oklahoma;* Kenneth C. Kaufman, "Blanket Flowers," "In a Border Town," "Llano Estacado," "The Passing Herd," from *Level Land;* Fania Kruger, "Messiah," from *Cossack Laughter;* "Passover Eve," from *The Tenth Jew;* Tom McNeal, "Return in October," "Killed in Action," from *Motley's the Only Wear;* Vaida Stewart Montgomery, "I Am Desert-Born," "Stampede," *Locoed and Other Poems,* "I Know Two Men," *Hail for Rain;* Whitney Montgomery, "Death Rode a Pinto Pony," "Storm at Night," *Hounds in the Hills,* "Ballad of Cynthia Ann Parker," *Joseph's Coat;* Patrick Dacus Moreland, "The Home-coming," "The Incredible Flower," "Seven Song," *Seven Song;* Lexie Dean Robertson, "Answer in the Night," from *Answer in the Night;* "Aftermath," "I Have Heard Whippoorwills," from *Red Heels,* "If I Had Been in Bethlehem," "My Sins and I," from *Acorn on the Roof;* David Russell, "Gifts," "Incomprehension," from *There Is No Night,* "Message from Tunisia," from *Sing With Me Now;* Arthur M. Sampley, "Ask of the Rain," "Of Those Who Wore the Wound Inside," from *Of the Strong and the Fleet,* "Desert Hunger," "Night Flight," "R.I.P.," from *This Is Our Time;* Goldie Capers Smith, "Aviator's Wife," "A Pilot to a Hunter," "Pilot-Song," "Shadows," "Teacher," from *Sword of Laughter;* Keith Thomas, "Children Through War," "Portrait of an American Village," from *Season of Shadow;* Fay M. Yauger, "Heritage," "I Remember," "Planter's Charm," from *Planter's Charm.* Application must be made to the Kaleidograph Press for any further use of these poems.

To D. Maitland Bushby, editor, and Maud E. Beghtol for "In Old Tucson," "Hopi Prayer," by Charles Beghtol, and to Mr. Bushby for "Yo-Tan-E-Ki," from *The Golden Stallion.*

To William Morrow and Company for "Beauty," by E-Yeh-Shure' (Louise Abeita), from *I Am a Pueblo Indian Girl.*

To Houghton Mifflin Company and to Henry Seidel Canby, literary executor for the estate of Mary Austin, for "Song for the Passing of a Beautiful Woman," "Papago Love Song," and "Lament of a Man for His Son," from *The American Rhythm.*

To *New Mexico* magazine for "Tent Rock," by Allison Ross (Mrs. Robert Anderson).

To *Poetry, A Magazine of Verse* for "Litany for New Mexico," by Mary Austin; "The Maid Who Became a Bear," by Ina Sizer Cassidy; "Litany," by Paul Horgan; "Prairie Pictographs," by Stanley Vestal (Walter S. Campbell).

To *Ranch Romances* for "Jack Potter's Courtin'," by S. Omar Barker.

To *The Saturday Evening Post* for "Petrified Forest," by S. Omar Barker. (Copyright, 1949, by The Curtis Publishing Company.)

To *Hollands* Magazine for "Los Penitentes," by S. Omar Barker.

To G. P. Putnam's Sons for "Quickened Earth," and "Ultimate Wound," by Isabel Harriss Barr, from *Sword Against the Breast;* for "The Cowboys' Christmas Ball," by "Larry" Chittenden, from *Ranch Verses.*

To Department of English, Texas Christian University, for "Upon This Mount," by William Barney, and "Circuit," by Thelma Breithaupt Cash.

To Meade and Company for "Prairie Days," by Don Blanding, from *Vagabond House.*

To Ben A. Botkin for "Tulsa, Oklahoma," by A. E. Browning, from *Folk-Say, A Regional Miscellany,* 1929, and "Pasó Por Aquí," by William Haskell Simpson, from *Folk-Say, A Regional Miscellany,* 1930.

To the University of Oklahoma Press for "Freedom Is a Word," by James Pipes, from *Ziba.*

To Alfred A. Knopf Company for the following poems by Witter Bynner: "A Dance for Rain," from *Selected Poems;* "Against the Cold," from *Against the Cold;* "Dead in the Philippines," "Prayer," and "Take Away the Darkness," from *Take Away the Darkness;* for "Ephemerides," by Edward Doro, from *The Boar and Shibboleth;* "Apology," "In the Harvest," and a sonnet from "Lady in April," by John McClure, from *Airs and Ballads.*

To the Dierkes Press, Chicago, Illinois, for "Clearing," "Country Auction," and "Winter Waking," by Irene Carlisle, from *Music by Lamplight.*

To St. Anthony Guild Press, Paterson, N. J., for "Mary," by Fray Angelico Chavez, from *Eleven Lady Lyrics.*

To Chapman and Grimes, Publishers, for "The Glory Trail," by Badger Clark, from *Sun and Saddle Leather.*

To Alice H. Rossin, daughter of Alice Corbin Henderson, for "Cundiyo," and "Juan Quintana," from *The Turquoise Trail*.

To Morton M. Cheney, of Albuquerque, for "New Mexico Spring," and "To a Greater Poet," by his wife, Ethel B. Cheney, from *New Language*.

To the Co-operative Publishing Company, Guthrie, Oklahoma, for "The Prairie Schooner," from *The Prairie Schooner,* by Edward Everett Dale.

To Grace Noll Crowell for "Red Earth," from *Flame in the Wind* (1930), and to Mrs. Crowell and Harper and Brothers for "The Aviator," from *The Wind-Swept Harp* (1946); for "The Human Heart," and "The Unbroken Rhythm," from *Light of the Years* (1936); for "The Poet," from *White Fire* (1934).

To the *New Mexico Quarterly* and John Gould Fletcher for "Songs of the Rio Grande"; to Mr. Fletcher for "Mexican Quarter," "Embarkation," and "Night Landing."

To Sam Giesey and *The Saturday Review of Literature* for "R.I.P. Indian Territory."

To Marilla Merriman Guild and the Paebar Company for "Clipped Wings," and "The Ocotilla in Bloom," from *The Old House Speaks and Other Poems*.

To *The Christian Science Monitor* for "The Hot Tamale Man," by Hazel Harper Harris, and for "Oklahoma Oil Field Pictures," by Lena Whitaker Blakeney.

To Dodd Meade Company for "Cerelle," by Margaret Bell Houston, from *Lanterns in the Dusk*.

To Random House for "Hands," by Robinson Jeffers, from *Dear Judas*.

To the *New Yorker* magazine for "Serous Spring," and "Remembering," by Reeve Spencer Kelley.

To The Caxton Printers, Ltd., for "The Shawled Model," by Phillips Kloss, from *Realization*.

To Houghton Mifflin Company for "Old Bill," by Henry Herbert Knibbs, from *Saddle Songs*.

To Frieda Lawrence and The Viking Press for "The American Eagle," by D. H. Lawrence, from *Birds, Beasts, and Flowers*.

To John McClure and *The American Mercury* for "In Bourbon Street."

To *Kaleidograph* magazine and the Tulsa *Tribune* for "Spring Song," and "For Oklahoma," by Dorothy McFarlane.

To Muna Lee and *The American Mercury* for "Prairie Sky."

To McGrew Printery, Phoenix, successors to the Republican Print Shop, for "Sheep Herding," by Sharlot M. Hall, from *Cactus and Pine*.

To R. T. MacBean, of the Republic National Bank, Dallas, Executor of the Estate of John A. Lomax, for "A Home on the Range," from *Cowboy Songs,* edited by John A. Lomax.

To David McKay Company for "At Sunrise," "Christmas in the Ozarks," "Place Flint Stones at My Roots," and "Sheep in a Hillside Churchyard," by Rosa Zagnoni Marinoni, from *Side Show*.

To the Press of James A. Decker, Prairie City, Illinois, for "Seventh Son," by Tom McNeal, from *Three Lyric Poets*.

To the Poetry Society of Oklahoma and The Times-Journal Publishing Company, Oklahoma City, for "Wonder," by Byron Chew; "In Peterborough Woods," "Mississippi Indians," by Anne McClure; for "Alibi," "Ne-Sha-Be," by Zoe A. Tilghman; 'I Love This Little Town," by Daisy Lemon Coldiron; from *State Anthology*.

To The Poetry Society of Texas, by David Russell, President, for "Sand Storm," by Patrick Dacus Moreland, from *Arrow Unspent*.

To Burton Publishing Company, Kansas City, Missouri, for "Black Gold," "In the Desert," "The Leader," and "Noon Trail," by Jennie Harris Oliver, from *Red Earth*.

To May Davison Rhodes, for "The Hired Man on Horseback," by Eugene Manlove Rhodes, from *Adventure Magazine* and *The Hired Man on Horseback*.

To Exposition Press for "An Ozark Ploughman," by Margaret Richter, from *Arkansas and Oklahoma Poets*.

To the *Atlantic Monthly* and the author for "At Woodstock," by Frances Ranson.

To Doubleday Doran for "Morning Walk—Santa Fe," by Lynn Riggs, from *The Iron Dish*.

To P. L. Turner Company, Dallas, for "The Boat That Never Sailed," by John P. Sjolander, from *Salt of the Earth*.

To the Regents of the University of California for "Singing Up the Corn," by Ruth Underhill, from *Singing for Power*.

Additional acknowledgments, as follows: Ruth Olive Angel and the Ponca City *News* for "Oklahoma's Will"; Henry T. Chambers for selections from *Young Man's Country;* the estate of Arthur Chapman for selections from *Cactus Center;* C. T. Davis, Jr., for "Other Dawns," from *Poems* by C. T. Davis; Mrs. Will Ferrell for "Not for Sale," from *Poems in Oil and Other Verse* by Will Ferrell;

Mary Carmack McDougal for "A Woman's Song," from *Songs from Oklahoma,* and for "The Oil Fire" and "The Phantom Round-up" by her sister and co-author, Violet McDougal, from *Wandering Fires;* William Brown Morrison for "A March Day in Oklahoma," from *Out in Oklahoma;* the estate of Alexander Posey and Crane Publishing Company, Topeka, Kansas, for selections from *Poems;* the estate of Ruth McEnery Stuart and D. Appleton Company for "Beauty-Land," from *Plantation Songs.*

This publication was made possible in part through a grant-in-aid allocated by a research committee at Texas Christian University to Mabel Major, from funds made available jointly by the Carnegie Foundation and that university. Neither the University nor the Foundation is responsible for the statements made in this book.

The following individuals, most of whom are associated with Southwestern institutions of learning, deserve our special thanks for assistance at one stage or another during the book's progress: Bertie Mothershead, Librarian, Texas Christian University; Grace Upchurch, Librarian, University of Arkansas; Jesse Rader, Librarian, University of Oklahoma; Ruth Russell, Librarian, University of New Mexico; Frederick Cromwell, Librarian, University of Arizona; Melvin T. Solve, Head, Department of English, University of Arizona; and Frances Gillmor, also of that Department, for reading the manuscript; Leonard Logan, Department of Government, University of Oklahoma, and Mary Hays Marable, Librarian, University of Oklahoma, for generous permission to use their large collections of Oklahoma poems; Walter John Lemke, Department of Journalism, University of Arkansas, for information concerning Arkansas poets and use of files; Irene Carlisle, Springdale, Arkansas; Robert Lee Morris and Earle Rudolph, Department of English, University of Arkansas; Walter Stanley Campbell and Jewell Wurtzbaugh, Department of English, University of Oklahoma; Frances Coldwell, Ft. Worth; Florence Shoemaker, Secretary to the Department of English, University of New Mexico, and the student assistants, Jack Boies and Dan Brosier.

MABEL MAJOR
T. M. PEARCE

Notes on Authors

WITH INDEX TO POEMS

LOUISE ABEITA (E-Yeh-Shure'), b. Laguna, N. M., 1926; ed. Univ. of N. M. Now teacher at Acomita Day School, N. M. Author in 1939 of *I Am A Pueblo Indian Girl,* sketches in verse and prose. Address: Isleta, N. M. (p. 11)

WALTER R. ADAMS, b. Purmela, Tex., 1897; ed. Baylor Normal. Books of poems: *The Dead Lie Down* (1934), *Bachelor's Poppy* (1940), *High to the Fruits* (1949). Address: Box 141, Ireland, Tex. (p. 159)

FRANCES ALEXANDER, b. Blanco, Tex., 1888; ed. Baylor Univ. (A.B.), Columbia Univ. (M.A.), Tex. Univ. Prof. of Eng., Tex. Coll. of Arts and Industries, 1925-1945. Past pres., Border Poets, Kingsville, Tex. Vols. of verse: *Seven White Birds* (1938), *Mother Goose on the Rio Grande* (1944), *Time At the Window* (1948, Poetry Book Award, Tex. Institute of Letters). Address: 1916 David Street, Austin, Tex. (pp. 237, 261)

JOHN HOUGHTON ALLEN, b. Austin, Tex., 1909; ed. private schools, five U. S. universities, Univ. of Mex., art school in Paris. Novels, short stories; poems: *The Poetry of John Houghton Allen.* Address: Box 855, Los Altos, Calif. (pp. 65, 66)

RUTH OLIVE ANGEL, b. Neosho, Mo.; ed. Central State Normal (Okla.), Univ. of Okla., Bread Loaf School. Poems in newspapers ("Oklahoma's Will," Ponca City *News,* August 16, 1935), mags., and anthologies (eds. Henry Harrison, Ted Malone). Address: Box 1454, Ponca City, Okla. (p. 125)

LOU ELLA ARCHER (Mrs. Harold Elliot), b. St. Paul, Minn., 1891. Been in and out of Phoenix since the age of five. Writes for Honolulu *Advertiser* and Phoenix papers. Vols. of poems: *Arms of Thought; Sonnets to the Southwest* (1930), *Canyon Shadows* (1932). Address: 3322 Country Club Manor, Phoenix, Ariz. (p. 43)

CARLOS ASHLEY, b. Cherokee, Tex., 1904; ed. Tex. Christian Univ. (A.B.), Cumberland Univ. (LL.B.). Vols. of poems: *These Texas Hills* (1941), *That Spotted Sow and Other Hill*

Country Ballads (1949). Poet laureate of Tex., 1949. Address: Llano, Tex. (p. 121)

MARY AUSTIN (Mrs. Mary Hunter Austin), b. Carlinville, Ill., 1868; ed. Blackburn Coll. (Ill.). Lived in Calif., Bakersfield, Lone Pine, Carmel; New York, trips abroad; came to Santa Fe in 1916. Recognized authority on Indian folklore. Non-fiction, novels, drama. Vols. of poems: *The American Rhythm* (1923, essay and re-expressions of Indian poems), *The Children Sing in the Far West* (1928). She died in 1934. (pp. 11, 12, 13, 252)

RUTH AVERITTE (Mrs. E. E.), b. Canadian, Tex.; ed. Univ. of Tex. (A.B., M.A.), Nat'l Training School, N. Y. Prose books; vols. of poems: *Salute to Dawn* (1936), *Cowboy Over Kiska* (1945). Past pres. Ft. Worth Poetry Soc.; vice pres., Am. Poetry League. Address: 2253 Fairmount Ave., Ft. Worth, Tex. (pp. 204, 238)

STANLEY E. BABB, b. Bristol, Eng., 1899; ed. Galveston, Tex., H. S., Univ. of Tex. Past vice pres., Tex. Institute of Letters. Book reviewer of *Galveston News* since 1923. Book of poems: *The Death of a Buccaneer* (1927, Book Award, Poetry Soc. of Tex.). Address: 4210 Ave. T., Galveston, Tex. (pp. 177, 179)

KARLE WILSON BAKER (Mrs. Thomas E.) b. Little Rock, Ark., 1878; ed. Little Rock Acad., Univ. of Chi., Columbia Univ. Member of Eng. Staff, Stephen F. Austin State Teachers Coll., 1925-34. Essays, journals, novels; poetry: *Blue Smoke* (1919), *Burning Bush* (1922), *Dreamers on Horseback* (1931). Past pres., Tex. Institute of Letters. Address: 1013 North St., Nacogdoches, Tex. (pp. 118, 161, 230, 268)

W. E. BARD (William Earl), b. Knightstown, Ind., 1892; at three came with parents to Tacquard Brothers ranch in Galveston Co., Tex.; ed. Southern Meth. Univ. (A.B.). Vice pres., Poetry Soc. of Tex. Vols. of poems: *A Little Flame Blown* (1933, Book Award, Poetry Soc. of Tex.), *Feather in the Sun* (1949). Address: 4614 Marcus St., Dallas, Tex. (pp. 174, 176)

S. OMAR BARKER, b. Beulah, N. M., 1894; ed. N. M. Highlands Univ. (A.B.). Poems in *Sat. Eve. Post, Country Gentleman, N. Y. Times,* anthologies, etc. and high school texts. Books of poems: *Vientos de las Sierras* (1924), *Buckaroo Ballads* (1928). Address: Sapello, N. M. (pp. 42, 47, 69, 70, 108)

WILLIAM BARNEY, b. Tulsa, Okla., 1916; ed. Tex. Christian Univ. Poems in magazines. Goethe Award, Poetry Soc. of Tex., for "The Garment," 1949; Margie B. Boswell Poetry Award for T. C. U. Ex-Students for "Upon This Mount," 1949. Address: 2325 Westbrook, Ft. Worth, Tex. (p. 241)

ISABEL HARRISS BARR (Mrs. John), b. Greenville, Tex., grew up in Okla. City; ed. Sorbonne, Paris; Coll. of New Rochelle, N. Y.; Columbia Univ. Books of poems: *Sword Against the Breast* (1935), *In the Beginning* (1945), *The Ship of Glass* (1946), *Let Time Relate* (1947). Address: 68 Valley Road, Larchmont, N. Y. (p. 235)

CHARLES ALEXANDER BEGHTOL, b. Macombe, Ill., 1869; ed. Univ. of Neb. Lived in Colorado, Nebraska, Utah, California. Made study of Southwest Indians, especially Hopi and Acoma. Books of Poems: *Goat Feathers, The Little Blue Flute* (1930). He died in 1940. (pp. 21, 55)

ALICE GILL BENTON, b. Mayville, Mich., 1890; ed. Univ. of Southern Calif. (A.B.), Mich. State Coll., Kan. State Teachers Coll., Univ. of N. M. Poems in anthologies; book in preparation. Address 26 Los Arboles Rd., Albuquerque, N. M. (p. 217)

LENA WHITAKER BLAKENEY (widow of B. B. Blakeney), b. West Fork, Ark.; ed. by father, Methodist missionary, Ark. and Okla. Ter. Poems in *Christian Science Monitor* ("Oklahoma Oil Field Patterns," March 28, 1932) and other journals; book of poems: *Ports of Call* (1926). Address: 601 N. W. 13th St., Okla. City 3, Okla. (pp. 184, 194)

DON BLANDING, b. Kingfisher, Okla. Ter., 1894; grew up in Enid and Lawton; ed. Chi. Art Inst. Served in World War I in A.E.F. Writing since then in Hawaii and U. S. Author of more than dozen vols. of verse, among them: *Vagabond House* (1928), *Songs of the Seven Seas* (1931), *Memory Room* (1935), *The Rest of the Road* (1937), *Today is Here* (1946). Address: Care Dodd, Mead and Co., 424 4th Ave., N. Y. (p. 134)

GEORGE BOND, b. 1903, Hillsboro, Tex.; ed. Southern Meth. Univ. (A.B., M.A.), Univ. of Mich. (Ph.D.); staff Eng. Dept., Southern Meth. Univ. since 1935. Ed. *Southwest Rev.,* 1925-27 co-ed. 1936-1941; advisory ed. since 1946. Poems in mags. and anthologies. Address: Southern Meth. Univ., Dallas, Tex. (p. 122)

MARGIE B. BOSWELL (widow of W. E. Boswell), b. Pueblo, Colo., 1875. Pres. of Am. Poetry League; past pres. of Ft. Worth Poetry Soc. Vols. of poems: *The Mockingbird and Other Poems* (1927), *The Upward Way* (1937), *Wings Against the Dawn* (1945). Address: 1516 W. Terrell Ave., Ft. Worth, Tex. (p. 120)

ROBERT LEE BROTHERS, b. Kokernot Ranch, Gonzales Co., Tex., 1908; ed. Baylor Univ. Worked for a time as cowhand in Tex. Panhandle. Lives now on his ranch in Gonzales Co. Book of poems: *Democracy of Dust* (1947). (pp. 205, 219)

A. E. BROWNING (Annie Eunice), b. Birmingham, Ala., 1907. Came to Okla. in 1913. Ed., Smith Coll. Poetry pub. in mags. and *The Southwest Scene* (1931), ed. B. A. Botkin. (p. 186)

ALICE BRILEY (Mrs. Albert L.), b. Vancouver, B. C., 1914; ed. Univ. of N. M. (A.B.) Poems in *Kaleidograph* ("The Piper," July, 1948, winner John Richard Moreland Memorial prize), *N. M. Quarterly, Epos,* and others. Vice pres., Albuquerque Branch, Nat. League of Am. Pen Women. Address: 1121 Major Ave., Albuquerque, N. M. (p. 240)

D. MAITLAND BUSHBY, b. Pueblo, Colo., Nov. 7, 1900; ed. State Teachers Coll., Flagstaff, Ariz., and Tempe, Ariz., Univ. of Ariz., State Univ. of Iowa, Columbia Univ. (B.Ed., Litt. D.). Member, Authors' League of Am. Poetry Soc. of London, Institute of Arts and Letters (Paris). Former ed. of *Palo Verde* and *Tom-Tom,* mags. of southwestern verse. Vols. of poems: *Don Felipe* (1929), *Tusayan* (1930), *Winds of the Desert* (1931), *Purple Sage* (1932), *April Will Return* (1937); ed., *The Golden Stallion,* anthology of southwestern verse (1930). Address: 1220 Glenn Ave., Fresno, Calif. (p. 22)

WITTER BYNNER, b. Brooklyn, N. Y., 1881; ed. Harvard (A.B.) Phi Beta Kappa poet, Harvard, Univ. of Calif., Amherst. Past pres. Poetry Soc. of Amer. Author of some twenty books of plays and poems, among them: *Young Harvard* (1907), *The Beloved Stranger* (1919), *Caravan* (1925), *Indian Earth* (1929), *Eden Tree* (1931), *Selected Poems* (1936), *Against the Cold* (1940), *Take Away the Darkness* (1947). Address: 342 Buena Vista Rd., Santa Fe, N. M. (pp. 25, 217, 237, 272, 273)

IRENE CARLISLE (Mrs. Jack A.), b. Decatur, Tex., 1908; ed. Tex. Christian Univ. (A.B.), Univ. of Ark. Lived in Ark.

since 1931, except for period during the war. Vol. of poems: *Music By Lamplight* (1945, Dierkes Press Book Award). Address: R. F. D. 4, Springdale, Ark. (pp. 146, 152, 238)

THELMA BREITHAUPT CASH (Mrs. Geo. L.), b. Powell, Tex., 1912; ed. Tex. Christian Univ. (A.B., M.A.). Vol. of poems: *No Silence Heard* (1937). Margie B. Boswell Poetry Award for T. C. U. Ex-Students in 1945 for poem "Circuit." Address: Crowley Road, Ft. Worth, Tex. (p. 218)

WALTER STANLEY CAMPBELL (see Stanley Vestal).

INA SIZER CASSIDY (widow of artist Gerald Cassidy), b. Sizer's Rancho, Bent Co., Colo.; ed. public school, private tutors, Columbia Univ. Ed. since 1931, of "Art and Artists" for the *N. M. Mag.* Poems in mags. and anthologies. Address: 924 Canyon Rd., Santa Fe, N. M. (p. 14)

HENRY T. CHAMBERS, b. Mt. Park, Okla., 1903; ed. Okla. Inst. of Tech., Univ. of Tulsa. Established Coronado Press, Bristow, Okla., in 1934, and pub. his own book of poems: *Young Man's Country.* (p. 31)

ARTHUR CHAPMAN, b. Rockford, Ill., 1873. Journalist and writer of Western stories and poems. Vols. of poems: *Out Where the West Begins and Other Western Verses* (1917), *Cactus Center* (1921). He died in 1935. (pp. 47, 51, 107)

FRAY ANGELICO CHAVEZ, b. Wagon Mound, N. M., 1910; ed. Duns Scotus Coll., Detroit, Franciscan Theol. Seminary, Oldenburg, Ind. Missionary to Indians in N. M. Army Chaplain with 77th Infantry Div., Hawaii, Guam, Leyte, 1943-44. Vice-pres., Catholic Poetry Soc. of Am., 1948-1950. Vols. of poetry: *Clothed With the Sun* (1939); *Eleven Lady Lyrics* (1945), *The Single Rose* (1948). Address: Franciscan Fathers, Peña Blanca, N. M. (pp. 73, 257, 264)

ETHEL B. CHENEY (Mrs. Morton M.), b. Warner, N. H., 1882; ed. Warner H. S. Member of Mavericks, Albuquerque, N. M. writers' group. Poems in mags. and in *Between the Book Ends,* ed. T. Malone (1942); two books: *Voices From the Fields* (1938), *New Language* (1941). Mrs. Cheney died in 1941. (pp. 71, 250).

BYRON CHEW, b. Oglesby, Okla., 1909; ed. Northeastern State Coll. of Okla. (A.B.), Univ. of Okla. (M.A.), Univ. of Puerto Rico. A regional director of the Okla. Poetry Soc. and author of *Thumb Prints* (1939). Address: 1802 S. Adams, Tucumcari, N. M. (pp. 151, 244)

LAWRENCE ("LARRY") CHITTENDEN, b. Montclair, N. J., 1862. In 1887 came to Tex. and bought a ranch near Anson. Known as the "poet-ranchman"; his book *Ranch Verses* (1893) in its 16th ed. at his death in 1934. (p. 93)

PEGGY POND CHURCH (Mrs. Fermor S.), b. Watrous, N. M., 1903; ed. Smith Coll. Before World War II lived at Los Alamos Ranch School, operated by her father and husband. Vols. of poems: *Familiar Journey* (1936), *Ultimatum for Man* (1946). Address: Rancho de Taos, N. M. (p. 223)

BADGER CLARK (Charles), b. Albia, Ia., 1883; ed. Dak. Wesleyan Univ. Four years on Ariz. ranch furnished material for most of the poems in *Sun and Saddle Leather* (1915) and *Grass Grown Trails* (1917). *Sky Lines and Wood Smoke* appeared in 1935. Poet laureate of S. D. Address: Mt. Coolidge Camp, Custer, S. Dak. (p. 103)

DAISY LEMON COLDIRON (Mrs. D. F.), b. near Marion, Ky. Came to Okla. Ter. in 1894, and later attended the Univ. of Okla. Books of poetry: *There Was a Garden* (1940), *Songs of Oklahoma* (1935), and *Who Touches This* (1940). A posthumous vol. in preparation. (pp. 18, 60, 267)

ALICE CORBIN (Mrs. William P. Henderson), b. St. Louis, Mo.; Assoc. ed., *Poetry, a Mag. of Verse,* 1912-16, and compiler with Harriet Monroe of *The New Poetry: An Anthology* (1917); also compiler of *The Turquoise Trail* (anthology of N. M. poetry) (1928). Lived in Santa Fe from 1916 until her death in 1949. Wrote prose and poetry; vols. of poems: *The Spinning Woman of the Sky* (1912), *Red Earth* (1920), *The Sun Turns West* (1933). (pp. 73, 74)

KATE McALPIN CRADY, b. Omega Plantation near Rolling Fork, Miss.; ed. Belhaven Coll. and Tex. Christian Univ. Lived in Ft. Worth, Tex., for a number of years. Vols. of Negro dialect poems: *Free Steppin* (1938), *Travlin Shoes* (1948). Address: Box 628, Gulfport, Miss. (pp. 164, 165)

A. L. CROUCH, b. Ft. Worth, Tex., 1914; ed. Tex. Christian Univ. (B.S.), Univ. of Tex. (M.A., LL.B.). Served with U. S. Army in Pacific, World War II. Poems in *Yank, Stars and Stripes;* vols: *This is Really Living* (1945), *China Sketchbook* (1946), *Ding How!* (1946). Address: 510 Burk Burnett Bldg., Ft. Worth, Tex. (pp. 48, 215)

GRACE NOLL CROWELL (Mrs. Norman H.), b. Inland, Ia., 1887; hon. Litt. D. Baylor Univ. Author of more than twenty books of poetry, among them: *White Fire* (1925), *Silver in the Sun* (1928), *Flame in the Wind* (1930), *Light of the Years* (1936), *The Radiant Quest* (1940), *The Wind Swept Harp* (1946), *Songs for Comfort* (1947), *The Crystal Fountain* (1948). Poet laureate of Tex., 1935-1937. Am. mother, 1938; one of ten outstanding Am. women, 1938. Address: 719 Lowell St., Dallas, Tex. (pp. 158, 200, 248, 256)

REID CROWELL, b. Alta, Ia., 1911; ed. Southern Meth. Univ., Dallas Art Inst. A son of Grace Noll Crowell and Norman Crowell. Book of poems: *The Old Intensities* (1949). Address: 719 Lowell St., Dallas, Tex. (p. 72)

EDWARD EVERETT DALE, b. Edmond, Okla., 1909; ed. Univ. of Okla. (A.B.) Harvard (M.A., Ph.D.). Pub. sixteen historical books, one vol. of poems: *The Prairie Schooner and Other Poems* (1929). Prof. of hist., Univ. of Okla. Address: 329 W. Main St., Norman, Okla. (p. 116)

C. T. DAVIS, b. Dardanelle, Ark., 1889; ed. Hendrix Coll., Conway, Ark. Ed. at eighteen of Dardanelle *Post-Dispatch*. For nearly thirty years assoc. ed. of the *Ark. Gazette*. Many of his poems printed in his editorial columns. Poet laureate of Ark. Vol. of poems: *Riders in the Sun* (1927). He died in 1945. (p. 239)

KATHARINE A. MURDOCK DAVIS (widow of John B. Davis), b. in Scotland; ed. private Scottish and English schools, Geneva Univ., Sorbonne, Heidelberg. With husband and son operated Bar-D Press, Siloam Springs, Ark., 1938-1941, publishing twenty-three books of verse. Among her own books: *Caedmon's Angel and Other Poems* (1910), *Broken Necklace* (1931). Address: 305 W. Harvard, Siloam Springs, Ark. (p. 153)

MARY ANNE DAVIS, b. Lexington, Ky., 1869; ed. Hamilton Coll. (Ky.), Univ. of Chi. On the staff of the English Dept. of the

Univ. of Ark. from 1893 until her death in 1939. Vol. of poems: *From My Window* (1939). (pp. 153, 247, 248)

FRANK DESPREZ. The editors have been unable to find any information on the author of the famous poem "Lasca." "Frank Desprez" may be a pseudonym. (p. 96)

EDWARD DORO, b. in North Dakota, 1910; ed. Univ. of S. Dak. (B.A.), Univ. of S. Calif. (M.A.). Traveled in England, France on Guggenheim Fellowship; National Inst. of Arts and Letters Award. Vols. of poetry: *Alms for Oblivion* (1931), *The Boar and the Shibboleth* (1932), *Shiloh* (1936), *Mr. Zenith* (1942). Address: 766 David Ave., Monterey, Calif. (p. 271)

GLENN WARD DRESBACH, b. Lanark, Ill., 1889; ed. Univ. of Wis. Lived in seven states including N. M., Tex., Ark., and Pan. Canal Zone. Wife, Beverley Githens, also a poet. Author of eleven vols. of poems including: *In Colors of the West* (1922), *The Enchanted Mesa* (1924), *Cliff Dwellings and Other Poems* (1926), *Star-Dust and Stone* (1928), *Collected Poems, 1914-48.* Address: Eureka Springs, Ark. (pp. 61, 124, 154, 192)

PAUL ELDRIDGE, b. Adrian, Mo., grew up in Okla.; ed Univ. of Okla. (B.A.), Harvard (M.A.), Univ. of Ia. (Ph.D.). Served in U. S. Navy, Medit. Area, World War II. Taught, Univ. of Okla. until 1944. Now prof. of English, Univ. of Nev. Poems in mags. and anthologies. Address: Univ. of Nev., Reno, Nev. (pp. 32, 250)

WILL FERRELL, b. Rushville, Ind., 1875; ed. high school, business coll. Lived in Midwest and southwestern states, Okla., N. M., Ariz. Poems in newspapers, collected in *Poems in Oil and Other Verse* (1919). Mr. Ferrell died in 1941. (p. 189)

JOHN GOULD FLETCHER, b. Little Rock, Ark., 1886; ed. Phillips Acad., Harvard Coll.; LL.D., Univ. of Ark. Lived much abroad and for several years in N. M. One of the originators of the Imagist school of poetry. Among his many vols.: *The Tree of Life* (1918), *Breakers and Granite* (1921), *Preludes and Symphonies* (1922), *Life is My Song* (1937) (autobiography), *Selected Poems* (1938, Pulitzer Poetry Award), *The Burning Mountain* (1946). Mr. Fletcher died in May, 1950. (pp. 38, 56, 145)

SAM GIESEY, b. Eagle Pass, Tex., 1908; ed. Tex. A.&M. Coll. (B.S. in Geol.), Univ. of Wis. Poems in the *Sat Rev. of Lit.* Address: 608 W. La. Ave., Midland, Tex. (p. 191)

EVERETT A. GILLIS, b. Cameron, Mo., 1914; ed. Tex. Christian Univ. (A.B., M.A.), Univ. of Tex. (Ph.D.). Served in the U. S. Army in the Pacific, World War II. Assoc. prof. of Eng., Tex. Tech. Coll. Vols. of poems: *Hello the House!* (1944), *Who Can Retreat?* (1944), *Sunrise in Texas* (1949). Address: 2207 8th St., Lubbock, Tex. (pp. 61, 157, 208)

HILTON ROSS GREER, b. Hawkins, Tex., 1879; ed. Univ. of Texas; hon. Litt. D., Austin Coll. For many years on staff of *Dallas Journal.* From its founding in 1921 until 1941, active pres., Poetry Soc. of Tex. and honorary pres. until death in 1949. Pres., Tex. Institute of Letters, 1942-44, and life member. Ed. anthologies of prose and poetry, among them *Voices of the Southwest* (1922); co-ed. with Florence Barnes, *New Voices of the Southwest* (1934). Among his own vols.: *A Prairie Prayer and Other Poems* (1912), *Ten and Twenty Aprils* (1935). (pp. 119, 173, 260)

MARILLA MERRIMAN GUILD, b. Gold Beach, Ore.; ed. State Teachers Coll., San Jose, Calif. (A.B.), Univ. of Ariz., Stanford Univ. Lived in Ore., Calif., Ariz.; year in Germany and France. Chairman, Rimers Club, Tucson, since 1923, which sponsors poetry prize contests, Univ. of Ariz. Vol. of poems: *The Old House Speaks* (1944). Address: 107 Olive Rd., Tucson, Ariz. (pp. 198, 199)

SHARLOT HALL, b. Prosser Creek, Kan., 1870. Came West in covered wagon in 1882 to Dewey, Ariz. Assoc. ed. of *Out West* 1906-7; Ariz. historian, 1909-12. Responsible for restoration of Old Governor's Mansion. Poet laureate of Ariz. Vol. of poems: *Cactus and Pine* (1910, 1924). She died in 1943. (p. 75)

HAZEL HARPER HARRIS (Mrs. John L. Brandner), b. Wesson, Miss.; ed. public schools of Tex., Univ. of Chi. Vol. of poems: *Wings of the Morning* (1930). Address: 6629 N. Washtenaw, Chi. 45, Ill. (p. 57)

CLYDE WALTON HILL, b. Austin, Tex., 1883; ed. Univ. of Tex. (A.B., LL.B.). Practiced law in Dallas; taught in North Dallas H. S. Vol. of poems: *Shining Trails* (1926). Treas., Poetry

Soc. of Tex., from its founding in 1921 until his death in 1932. (p. 259)

CAREY HOLBROOK, b. Bolivar, Mo., 1885; ed. Prep Dept. Univ. of Ark. Moved to N. M. in 1922. Ed. and columnist, *Health City Sun,* Albuquerque, 1930-1945. Vol. of poetry: *Life Goes On* (1937). Address: 313 N. Dartmouth, Albuquerque, N. M. (p. 64)

VERA HOLDING, b. San Saba, Tex., 1894; ed. Daniel Baker Coll., Amer. Conservatory of Music. Scholarship, 1941, McDowell Colony. Vols. of poems: *Prairie Nautilus* (1936), *Prairie Moods* (1938), *Prairie Brand* (1946). Address: Tipton, Okla. (pp. 117, 126)

PAUL HORGAN, b. Buffalo, N. Y., 1903; ed. N. M. Military Institute; librarian there since 1926 except for war service, 1942-46; advanced to lt. col., awarded Legion of Merit. Primarily known as a novelist and playwright; poems in mags. and anthologies, as *The Turquoise Trail* (1928). Address: Roswell, N. M. (p. 257)

BOYCE HOUSE, b. Piggott, Ark., 1896; ed. public schools of Ark., Miss., Mo., Ariz., Tex., Tenn. Known as humorist and historian; appears on radio, television programs; newspaper columnist. Author of ten books of prose and vols. of poems: *Texas Rhythms* (1936), *Texas Rhythms and Other Poems* (1950). Address: 3329 Park Ridge, Ft. Worth, Tex. (pp. 138, 139)

MARGARET BELL HOUSTON, granddaughter of Gen. Sam Houston, b. Houston, Tex.; ed. St. Mary's Coll., Columbia Univ., Am. Acad. of Dra. Arts. Author of nine novels, books of poems: *Prairie Flower* (1907), *The Singing Heart* (1926, Book Award, Poetry Soc. of Tex.), *Lanterns in the Dusk* (1930). Address: 16 W. 74th St., N. Y.; 3648 Maplewood, Dallas, Tex. (pp. 127, 180)

ROBINSON JEFFERS, b. Pittsburgh, Pa., 1887; ed. Occidental Coll. (A.B., D. Litt.), Univ. of Southern Calif. Med. Sch., Univ. of Zurich (Switzerland), Univ. of Southern Calif. (L.H.D.). Member Nat'l Institute of Arts and Letters, Am. Acad. of Arts and Letters. Summer residence in Taos, N. M., 1930's. Among his vols. of poems: *Tamar* (1924), *The Women of Point Sur* (1927), *Cawdor* (1928), *Dear Judas* (1929), *Give Your Heart to the Hawks* (1933), *Solstice* (1935), *Such Counsels You Gave Me*

(1937), *Selected Poetry* (1938), *Be Angry at the Sun* (1941). Address: Tor House, Carmel, Calif. (p. 20)

SIDDIE JOE JOHNSON, b. Dallas, Tex., 1905; grew up in Corpus Christi; ed. Tex. Christian Univ. (A.B.), La. State Univ. (B.S. in Lib. Sci.). Children's Librarian, Dallas Public Library. Author of juveniles, vols of poems: *Agarita Berry* (1933), *Gallant the Hour* (1945). Address: 1004 N. Carroll, Dallas, Tex. (pp. 180, 233)

WILLARD (SPUD) JOHNSON, b. Mt. Vernon, Ill., 1897; ed. Colo. State Teachers Coll., Univ. of Colo., Univ. of Calif. At one time on staff of *New Yorker, Sunset Mag.,* ed. of *Laughing Horse.* Has lived in Taos, N. M., since 1922. Book of poems: *Horizontal Yellow* (1935). Address: Taos, N. M. (pp. 79, 242, 243)

KENNETH KAUFMAN, b. Leon, Kan., 1887; moved to Okla. 1898; ed. Southwestern State Teachers Coll. (Okla.), Univ. of Okla. (A.B., M.A.). From 1929 until death in 1945, prof. of mod. lang., Univ. of Okla., and co-ed. of *Books Abroad.* Vol. of poetry: *Level Land, A Book of Western Verse* (1935, co-winner of *Kaleidograph* Book Award). (pp. 29, 63, 114, 115)

REEVE SPENCER KELLEY, b. Willoughby, Ohio, 1912. Except for grade school and three years of high school, self-educated during long illness. Lived in twenty-five states—longest in Ohio, Colo., Fla., N. M. Writer-caretaker of Ernie Pyle Library, Albuquerque, N. M. Contrib. to: *New Yorker, Sat. Eve. Post,* and other periodicals. Address: 902 Girard, Albuquerque, N. M. (p. 232)

PHILLIPS KLOSS, b. Webster Grove, Mo., 1902; ed. Univ. of Calif. (A.B.). Married to Gene Kloss, well known etcher and painter. Vols. of poetry: *Arid* (1925), *The Cloudburst* (1937), *Realization* (1942). Addresses: Taos, N. M., and Berkeley, Calif. (p. 78)

FARONA KONOPAK (Mrs. Lothar T.), b. Philadelphia, 1895; ed. in public schools and by tutors. Courier on the Santa Fe Indian Detour for a number of years. Book of poems: *Adobe in Sunlight* (1935). Address: 605 Camino del Monte Sol, Santa Fe, N. M. (p. 77)

HENRY HERBERT KNIBBS, b. Niagara Falls, Ontario, Canada, 1874, of American parents; ed. Ridley Coll. (Ont.), Harvard.

Writer of Western stories and poems. Lived in Calif., Ariz., N. M. Among books of poems: *Songs of the Outlands* (1914), *Songs of the Trail* (1920), *Saddle Songs* (1922), *Songs of the Lost Frontier* (1930). He died in 1945. (p. 105).

FANIA KRUGER (Mrs. Sam), b. Sevastopol, Crimea, Russia, 1893; ed. gymnasia in Sevastopol; Ft. Worth, Tex., H. S.; Wichita Falls Junior Coll., sum. sessions Harvard, Univ. of Colo., Columbia Univ. Books of poems: *Cossack Laughter* (1937), *The Tenth Jew* (1949). Poetry Soc. of Am. annual award for poem "The Passover." Address: 1305 Buchanan, Wichita Falls, Tex. (pp. 220, 254)

D. H. LAWRENCE, b. Eastwood, Eng., 1885; ed. Univ. Coll., Nottingham. He and his wife Frieda lived from 1922-1925 on a ranch near Taos, N. M. Better known as a novelist, he published ten vols. of poems, among them: *Love Poems and Others* (1913), *Birds, Beasts, and Flowers* (1923), *Collected Poems* (1928), *Last Poems* (1933). Died in Italy in 1930; his ashes brought back to the Del Monte (N. M.) ranch where Frieda Lawrence now lives. (p. 81)

MARCELLE CHANCELLOR LEATH (Mrs.), b. Mangum, Okla., 1915; ed. Okla. Coll. for Women, Okla. A. & M. Has lived in Okla., La., and Ark. Vol. of poems: *Awake in the Night* (1948). Address: 110 Prospect, Camden, Ark. (pp. 150, 246)

MUNA LEE, b. Raymond, Miss., 1895; ed. Blue Mt. Coll., Univ. of Miss. (B.S.), Univ. of Okla. Active in political and international affairs. Poems in *New Yorker, Am. Mercury, Southwest Review*. Poetry vol.: *Sea Change*. Address: c/o Dept. of State, Washington, D. C. (pp. 198, 249)

THERESE LINDSEY (Mrs.), b. Tyler, Tex., 1870; ed. San Marcos Normal, Univ. of Chicago, Columbia Univ. Initiated the organization of the Poetry Soc. of Tex. in 1921 and is hon. vice-pres. for life. Vols. of poems: *Blue Norther* (1925), *Cardinal Flower* (1934), *Collected Poems*. Donor of the Old South Prize of The Poetry Soc. of Tex. Address: Box 2016, Tyler, Tex. (pp. 160, 187, 199)

JOHN A. LOMAX, b. Goodman, Miss., 1867; came with parents to Tex., 1869; ed. Univ. of Tex. (A.B.), Harvard (M.A.). Lived most of his life in Tex., but travelled widely collecting folk ballads for books, and records for Lib. of Congress. Among his books: *Cowboy Songs* (1910), *Songs of the Cattle Trail and Cow Camps* (1918), *Our Singing Country* (with Alan Lomax) (1941), *The Adventure of a Ballad Hunter* (1947). He died in 1949. (p. 87)

HANIEL LONG (Clark), b. Rangoon, Burma, 1888, of Am. parentage; came to U. S., 1891; ed. Harvard (A.B.). Member of the Eng. staff of Carnegie Institute of Tech., 1910-1929, when he moved to Santa Fe, N. M. Organized Writer's Editions, 1933-1939. Among vols. of poems: *Atlantides* (1933), *Interlinear to Cabeza de Vaca* (1936), *The Power Within Us* (1943), *The Grist Mill* (1945). Address: Box 952, Santa Fe, N. M. (pp. 21, 230, 231)

LILITH LORRAINE (Mary M. Wright), b. Corpus Christi, Tex., 1894; ed. convent and Univ. of Calif., Univ. of Ariz., Univ. of Mex. Ed. of anthologies, author of books of poems: *Banners of Victory* (1937), *Beyond Bewilderment* (1942), *The Day Before Judgment* (1944), *Let the Patterns Break* (1947). Ed. of *Different*. Address: Rogers, Ark. (pp. 50, 203)

NORMAN MACLEOD, b. Salem, Ore., 1906; ed. Univ. of Iowa, Univ. of N. M. (A.B.), Univ. of Southern Calif., Univ. of Okla., Teachers Coll., Columbia (M.A.). Lived in both East and West of U. S., France, Holland, England, U. S. S. R. Author of poetry: *Horizons of Death* (1934), *Thanksgiving Before November* (1936), *We Thank You All the Time* (1941), *A Man in Mid-Passage* (collected poems, 1930-1947), *Adam's Off Ox* (in preparation). Address: Apt. 38, 107 W. 109 St., New York 25, N. Y. (pp. 22, 23, 236)

ROSA ZAGNONI MARINONI (Mrs. L. A. Passarelli), b. Bologna, Italy, 1891. Founder of the Univ. Poets, of Fayetteville, Ark., where her husband is a member of the Mod. Lang. Dept. of the Univ. Among her poetry vols.: *Behind the Mask* (1927), *Red Kites and Wooden Crosses* (1929), *Side Show* (1938). Address: Villa Rosa, Fayetteville, Ark. (pp. 149, 214, 260)

WASHINGTON MATTHEWS, b. Killiney, Ireland, 1843; came to U. S. in infancy; ed. Univ. of Ia. Surgeon in U. S. Army, 1864-1889. Contrib. to ethnological and philological studies of Navajos. Best known works: *The Mountain Chant: a Navajo Ceremony* (1887), *Navajo Myths, Prayers and Songs* (1907); translations reprinted by G. Cronyn, *Path on the Rainbow* (1918, 1934),

M. Astrov, *The Winged Serpent* (1946). Washington Matthews died in 1905. (p. 7)

ANNE McCLURE (Mrs. John Alexander), b. Austin, Tex., 1865, grew up in Ark.; ed. Univ. of Ark., studied voice in Boston, N. Y., Florence, Italy. Lived in Okla. from her marriage in 1902 until her death in 1938. Her stepson, John McClure, also a poet. Poems pub. in mags. and anthologies. (pp. 27, 28)

JOHN McCLURE, b. Ardmore, Okla., 1893; ed. Univ. of Okla. (A.B.), studied in Paris, Fr. Served in the 304th Cav. in World War I. Has lived in New Orleans since 1919 where he is head copy-reader of the *Times Picayune*. Vol. of poems: *Airs and Ballads* (1918). Ed. *Stag's Hornbook* (1919), an anthology of convivial verse; reissue in 1943 with war poems added, selected by William Rose Benet. Address: *Times Picayune,* New Orleans. (pp. 127, 247, 249, 265)

MARY CARMACK McDOUGAL (Mrs. Ivar Axelson), b. Sel-mar, Tenn.; ed. Kidd-Key, Unv. of Okla., Columbia Univ. Grew up in Sapulpa, Okla. Better known for her play *Life Begins* (1932), co-author with her sister of a book of poems *Wandering Fires* (1925). Address: 1225 Alhambra Circle, Coral Gables 34, Fla. (p. 131)

VIOLET McDOUGAL, b. Selmar, Tenn., 1898; ed. Kidd-Key, Univ. of Mo., Univ. of Okla., Columbia Univ. Grew up in Sapulpa, Okla. First poet laureate of Okla. (1923-1931). Co-author of *Wandering Fires* (1925). (pp. 111, 188)

DOROTHY McFARLANE (Mrs. Joe), b. Belfast, Ireland, 1905. Lived in the U. S. since 1916, and in Okla. since 1926. Poems published in mags. Address: 2705 N. W. 45th St., Okla. City, Okla. (pp. 129, 130)

TOM H. McNEAL, b. Gonzales, Tex.; ed. Univ. of Tex. (A.B., B.J., M.A., Ph.D.), Columbia. During World War I served in the U. S. Army in France. Lived in Tex. until 1946 when he went to the Univ. of Ala. as prof. of Eng. Author: *Motley's the Only Wear* (1942), and with two other poets of *Shadow on Stone* (1942). Address: 20 Audubon Place, Tuscaloosa, Ala. (pp. 212, 213, 236)

VAIDA STEWART MONTGOMERY (Mrs. Whitney), b. Childress Co., Tex., 1888; ed. public schools of Tex., Metropolitan

Business Coll., Dallas. Author of handbooks, a reference work, *A Century With Tex. Poets and Poetry* (1934); co-ed. with her husband of four books and of the Kaleidograph Press. Author, poetry: *Locoed and Other Poems* (1930), *Hail for Rain* (1948, Poetry Book Award, Tex. Institute of Letters). Address: 624 N. Vernon Ave., Dallas 8, Tex. (pp. 62, 245, 262)

WHITNEY MONTGOMERY, b. Navarro Co., Tex., 1877; ed. public schools. Editor and publisher of *Kaleidograph, A Nat'l Mag. of Verse,* and co-ed. with wife of Kaleidograph Press. Ed. of poetry anthology, *The Road to Texas* (1940), co-ed. with wife of four books. Author, poetry: *Corn Silks and Cotton Blossoms* (1928), *Brown Fields and Bright Lights* (1930), *Hounds in the Hills* (1934), *Joseph's Coat* (1946, Poetry Book Award, Tex. Institute of Letters). Past pres., Tex. Institute of Letters; hon. vice-pres., Poetry Soc. of Tex. Address: 624 N. Vernon Ave., Dallas 8, Tex. (pp. 17, 67, 254)

PATRICK DACUS MORELAND, b. Unaka, N. C., 1897; lived in Okla. from 1900-1913, when he moved to Tex.; ed. Southern Meth. Univ. (A.B.). Among his books of poems: *Arrow Unspent* (1931, Book Award, Poetry Soc. of Tex.), *Slumber at Noon* (1934, Kaleidograph Book Award), *Seven Song* (1936). Address: Tex. Restaurant Assoc., Austin, Tex. (pp. 46, 133, 173, 244)

WILLIAM BROWN MORRISON, b. Lexington, Ky., 1877; ed. Washington and Lee (A.B.), hon. Litt. D., Austin Coll., Univ. of Okla. (M.A.). Prof. of hist., Southeastern Teachers Coll., Durant, Okla. Author of historical books; vol. of poems: *Out in Oklahoma* (1934). Address: Southeastern Teachers Coll., Durant, Okla. (p. 128)

BERTA HART NANCE, b. near Albany, Tex., 1883; ed. Albany public schools and Reynolds Presbyterian Acad.; lived in West Tex. until she moved to Ariz. some twelve years ago. Vols. of poetry: *The Round-up* (1926), *Flute in the Distance* (1935), *Lines from Ariz.* (1938). Address: 3461 S. Clark Ave., Tucson, Ariz. (pp. 42, 52, 112, 113, 251)

JENNIE HARRIS OLIVER (Mrs. Lloyd), b. Lowell, Mich.; came to Okla. in 1898; ed. privately. Lived for a number of years in Fallis, Okla. Better known as a writer of fiction; pub. one book of poems: *Red Earth* (1934). She died in 1942. (pp. 59, 62, 132, 185)

JAMES PIPES, b. Natchez, Miss. For ten years clerked in "Forty-Acres Store" in swamplands of La. Studied at Univ. of Okla. Poems in *Southwest Review* and in a vol. *Ziba,* illust. by Edith Mahier and pub. by Univ. of Okla. Press, 1943. Address: 721 Peters, Norman, Okla. (p. 167)

ALEXANDER LAWRENCE POSEY, b. 1873 near Eufaula, Ind. Ter. Mother, Creek Indian; father, Scotch-Irish; ed. Bacone Coll., Muskogee, Okla. Wrote Eng.-Ind. dialect articles and poems under the name of Chinnubbie Harjo. He was drowned in 1908. His widow, Mrs. Minnie H. Posey, ed. *The Poems of Alexander Lawrence Posey* (1910). (pp. 15, 16)

FRANCES RANSON (Mrs. Lowell Dunham), b. Longdale, Okla., 1913; ed. Central State Coll. (A.B.), Univ. of Okla. (M.A.). Teaches in dept. of education, Univ. of Okla. "At Woodstock" in *Atlantic Monthly* June, 1949. Address: 439 Chautauqua, Norman, Okla. (p. 240)

NANCY RICHEY RANSON (Mrs.), b. Berryville, Va.; ed. private and public Va. schools; Univ. of Ariz. Lived in many states including Ariz, N. M., and Tex. Tex. poet laureate, 1941-43. Feature writer for the *Dallas News.* Among her books of verse: *Texas Evening* (1936), *My Neighbor's Garden and Mine* (1939). Address: 6151 Vanderbilt Ave., Dallas 14, Tex. (p. 50)

EUGENE MANLOVE RHODES, b. Tecumseh, Neb., 1869; came with his family to N. M. in 1881. After school days, became teacher, cowboy, and rancher. Best known as a novelist; collection of his poems in *The Little World Waddies,* prepared for printing by William Hutchinson (1946). Best known poem "Hired Man on Horseback," which gave title to biography by his widow. "Gene" Rhodes died in 1934. (p. 99)

MARGARET R. RICHTER; ed. Stanford Univ. (A.B., M.A., Ph.D.). Instructor in Eng., Univ. of Ark., 1929-35. Poems in mags. and anthologies, including *Kaleidograph* and *Ark. and Okla Poets* (1936). Address: 723 S. Bronson Ave., Los Angeles 5, Calif. (p. 150)

LYNN RIGGS, b. near Claremore, Ind. Ter., 1899; ed. Okla. Military Acad. and Univ. of Okla. Lived for a time in N. M. Primarily a dramatist, having written among other plays *Green*

Grow the Lilacs on which the musical play *Oklahoma* based. Book of poems: *The Iron Dish* (1930). Address: 1 Christopher St., N. Y. (p. 77)

LEXIE DEAN ROBERTSON (Mrs. James F.), b. Lindale, Tex.; ed. N. Tex. State Teachers Coll., Howard Payne Coll. (A.B.), Univ. of Okla., Univ. of Chi. Vols. of poems: *Red Heels* (1928), *I Keep a Rainbow* (1932), *Acorn on the Roof* (1939), *Answer in the Night* (1948). Past pres. of the Tex. Institute of Letters; poet laureate of Texas, 1939-1941. Address: Rising Star, Tex. (pp. 161, 193, 221, 255, 266)

ALLISON ROSS (Mrs. Robert Anderson, Jr.), b. Baltimore, Md.; ed. Goucher Coll. Member of Mavericks, Albuquerque, and Poetry Soc. of Am. Poems in *Sat. Eve. Post, Sat. Rev. of Lit., Kaleidograph,* etc. Address: 3410 Monte Vista, Albuquerque, N. M. (p. 76)

GRACE ROSS (widow of Edwin J.), b. near Tyler, Tex.; ed. N. Tex. State Teachers Coll., Carver Chiropractic Coll. Past pres., Ft. Worth Poetry Soc.; co-author (with Mabel M. Kuykendall) *Divert the Interim* (1940), author, *Journey out of Night* (1946); ed. (with Mabel M. Kuykendall) *Out Where the West Begins, an Anthology of Fort Worth Authors* (1949). Address: 929 S. Lake St., Ft. Worth 4, Tex. (pp. 159, 253)

DAVID RUSSELL, b. Fairfield, Tex., 1902; ed. Southern Meth. Univ. (A.B.), Carnegie Inst. of Tech. (M.A.); member of dept. of speech, Southern Meth. Univ. Poet laureate of Tex., 1945-1947. Pres. of Poetry Soc. of Tex. since 1941. Vols. of poems: *There Is No Night* (1942), *Sing With Me Now* (1945, Poetry Book Award, Tex. Institute of Letters), *The Silver Fawn* (1946). Address: 2945 Stanford, Dallas, Tex. (pp. 222, 243, 263)

ARTHUR M. SAMPLEY, b. Leander, Tex., 1903; ed. Univ. of Tex. (A.B., M.A., Ph.D.), Columbia Univ. (B.S. in L.S.). Served in Air Force in World War II. Vols. of poems: *This is Our Time* (1943), *Of the Strong and the Fleet* (1947, Kaleidograph Book Award, Tex. Institute of Letters Poetry Book Award). In 1939 co-winner of Maxwell Anderson Verse Drama Award. Past pres., Tex. Institute of Letters; vice pres., Poetry Soc. of Tex. Head librarian, North Texas State Coll. Address: Box 5263, N. T. Station, Denton, Tex. (pp. 60, 203, 215, 219, 268)

WILLIAM HASKELL SIMPSON, b. Lawrence, Kan., 1858; ed. Univ. of Kan. With Santa Fe Railway from 1881. Vol. of poems of N. M. and Ariz.: *Along Old Trails* (1929). He died in 1933. (p. 45)

JOHN P. SJOLANDER, b. Hudiksvall, Sweden, 1851. Came to Galveston, Tex., in 1870. Lived in Cedar Bayou, Tex., from 1878 until death in 1939. Known as the "Dean of Tex. Poets." Vol. of poems: *Salt of the Earth and Sea* (1928). (p. 174)

GOLDIE CAPERS SMITH (Mrs. Hugh L.), b. E. Feliciana Parish, La.; lived in Tex. from infancy until 1930; ed. Southern Meth. Univ. (A.B.), Univ. of Tulsa. Her husband, an aviator, d. 1947. Vols. of poems: *Sword of Laughter* (1932), *Gardens Under the Snow* (1942, co-winner, Kaleidograph Book Award). Address: 4704 E. 8th St., Tulsa, Okla. (pp. 49, 200, 201, 258, 267)

RICHARD LEON SPAIN, b. near Mangum, Okla., 1916; ed. Bentonville, Ark., H. S. Lived in Ark and Okla. Poem "A Hill Mother" included in Thos. Moult's *The Best Poems of 1935*. Vols: *Travelers of the Night* (1938), *Rock and Cumulus* (1942). Address: R. 1. Bentonville, Ark. (pp. 151, 202)

HERBERT JOSEPH SPINDEN, b. 1879; Am. anthropologist, interpreter of culture of pre-European Western hemisphere. Author of technical studies, "An Essay on American Indian Poetry," and translations of Indian verse, in *Songs of the Tewa* (1933). Address: The Brooklyn Museum, Eastern Parkway, Brooklyn 17, N. Y. (p. 13)

THOMAS WOOD STEVENS, b. Oregon, Ill., 1880; ed. Armour Inst. of Tech., Chi. Lived in Midwest, Pa., Calif., France, Belgium, N. M. Member, Cliff Dwellers, Chi.; Players, N. Y. Author: plays, pageants, poetry. Narrative poem, *Westward Under Vega* (1938). Mr. Stevens died in 1942. (p. 44)

RUTH McENERY STUART, b. La., 1856. Spent her married life in Ark. Wrote of the Creole and Negro in prose stories and poems. She died in N. Y. in 1917. (p. 163)

ALAN SWALLOW, b. Powell, Wyo., 1915; ed. Univ. of Wyo. (A.B.), La. State Univ. (M.A., Ph.D.). Taught Univ. of N. M., Univ. of Denver. Author, editor, and publisher of poetry. Author:

The Practice of Poetry (1942), *The Remembered Land* (1946), *War Poems* (1948). Address: Univ. of Denver, Denver 10, Colo. (p. 213)

KEITH THOMAS, b. Washington Co., Kan., 1911; ed. Univ. of Neb. (A.B., M.A.). Came to Tex. in 1934, and living at McAllen when he entered the army in 1943. Served in France in the 80th Division of the Third Army and was killed in action Nov. 10, 1944. Poems printed in leading mags. and newspapers compiled and ed. by his parents in the vol. *Season of Shadow* (1946). (pp. 222, 223)

MARGARET FOX THOMPSON (Mrs. Beverly V., Jr.), b. Frankill, Tex., 1925; ed. Tex. State Coll. for Women (A.B.). Poems in *Daedalian Quarterly* and *Out Where the West Begins,* an anthology. Address: 100 Penn, Ft. Worth, Tex. (pp. 211, 212)

NATHAN HOWARD (JACK) THORP, b. N. Y. City, 1876; ed. St. Paul's School, Concord, N. H. Came West in his teens, ranching, engineering, N. M. First collected cowboy songs in 1889; first publisher of cowboy ballads. Vol.: *Songs of the Cowboys* (Estancia, N. M., 1908); rev. ed., Houghton Mifflin, 1921. "Jack" Thorp's home was in Albuquerque, where he died in 1940. (pp. 88, 89, 90, 91, 109)

ZOE A. TILGHMAN (widow of Wm. M. Tilghman), b. Greenwood Co., Kan., 1880; ed. Univ. of Okla., Okla. Central Coll. (A.B.). Author of four prose books and vol. of poems: *Prairie Winds* (1930). Founder and past pres., Poetry Soc. of Okla.; past pres., Okla. Writers. Address: 3130 N. Barnes, Okla. City 6, Okla. (pp. 29, 30, 114, 137)

RUTH M. UNDERHILL, b. Ossining, N. Y., 1890; ed. Vassar (A.B.), London School of Economics, Columbia Univ. (Ph.D.). Traveled for Indian Service, every state in the Union; lived year or more in England, Italy, Spain. Vol. of interpretation and poetry: *Singing for Power* (1938, 1946). Address: Dept. of Anthropology, Denver 10, Colo. (p. 8)

STANLEY VESTAL (Walter Stanley Campbell), b. Severy, Kan., 1887; ed. Southwestern State Normal Sch., Weatherford, Okla., Rhodes Scholar, Merton Coll., Oxford (A.B., M.A.). Except for service in World War I, he has been a member of the Eng. faculty of the Univ. of Okla. since 1915. In addition to many historical and biographical books and one novel, he has a vol. of poems: *Fandango, Ballads of the Old West* (1927). Address: Dept. of Eng., Univ. of Okla., Norman, Okla. (p. 123)

CHARLES WILEY, b. Santa Rosa, N. M., 1922; ed. Univ. of N. M. (A.B.), Columbia Univ. (M.A.). Served in U. S. Navy, South Pacific, 1942-1945; taught Univ. of Ariz. Poetry in mags. and *Anthology of American College Poetry*. Address: Tucson, Ariz., or Santa Rosa, N. M. (p. 216)

FAY YAUGER, b. Weiser, Id., 1902; ed. Lindenwood Coll. (Mo.). Lived in Wichita Falls, Tex., since 1923. Title poem of her vol., *Planter's Charm* (1935) won the Poetry Soc. of Am. Annual Award in 1933. (pp. 58, 146, 269, 270)

Date Due

FEB 2 6 1951			
JUN 2 1954			